Praise for *Staunch*

'A fun and uplifting memoir'
Cosmopolitan

'Warm and funny and unpretentious and wise.'
Holly Bourne, author of *Am I Normal Yet?*

'Laced with many laugh-out-loud moments'
Sunday Post

Eleanor Wood is the author of novels *My Secret Rockstar Boyfriend* and *Becoming Betty*, both about music and growing up. She works as a journalist/editor, and is the co-founder of the fanzine *I Am Not Ashamed*. She lives in Brighton, where she has a pink kitchen and a lot of feelings.

STAUNCH

ELEANOR WOOD

ONE PLACE. MANY STORIES

HQ
An imprint of HarperCollins*Publishers* Ltd
1 London Bridge Street
London SE1 9GF

www.harpercollins.co.uk

HarperCollins*Publishers*
1st Floor, Watermarque Building, Ringsend Road
Dublin 4, Ireland

This edition 2022

1

First published in Great Britain by
HQ, an imprint of HarperCollins*Publishers* Ltd 2020

ISBN: 978-0-00-832572-5

MIX
Paper from
responsible sources
FSC
www.fsc.org   FSC® C007454

This book is produced from independently certified FSC™ paper
to ensure responsible forest management.

For more information visit: www.harpercollins.co.uk/green

Typeset by Palimpsest Book Production Ltd, Falkirk, Stirlingshire

Printed and Bound in the UK using 100% Renewable Electricity at
CPI Group (UK) Ltd

For Pansy, Rose and Thistle

'But, you see, in dealing with me, the relatives didn't know that they were dealing with a staunch character – and, I tell you, if there's anything worse than a staunch woman . . .

S-T-A-U-N-C-H: there's nothing worse, I'm telling you.'

Edith 'Little Edie' Bouvier Beale,
Grey Gardens

staunch
adjective
1. very loyal and committed in attitude
   synonyms: stalwart, loyal, faithful, trusty, committed, devoted, dedicated, dependable, reliable, steady, constant, hard-working, vigorous, stable, firm, steadfast, redoubtable, resolute, unswerving, unwavering, unhesitating, unfaltering
   "a staunch supporter of the cause"

2. of strong or firm construction
   "these staunch walls could withstand attack by cannon"

Present Day

'Well, cheers, girls. We made it! Here's to the Go-ers.'

The four of us clink glasses. My cocktail tastes of pure alcohol and sugar, it's called a 'Go-go Goa' and it's made with fenny, the local moonshine that – I think – comes from cashew nuts. We arrived in the early hours of the morning and this is our first early afternoon cocktail.

I'm on the beach, on the first day of a girls' holiday. I'm wearing shorts and a bikini top, and successfully managing to skip cold and grey January back home. The sea is there, right in front of me – not only a picture-perfect sparkling bright blue, but warm and inviting. I've already been straight in for a swim. The sand is warm under our feet and the sun on our faces is heavenly. We are jetlagged and slightly frazzled after a long journey, but the excitement is palpable.

There are dogs and cows wandering around the beach and ladies in saris trying to sell us things on every corner. We are in India.

Specifically, we are in a beach shack strewn with fairy

lights and residual Christmas decorations, sitting on picnic chairs. A sort of Indian-style mariachi duo wearing matching Hawaiian shirts and cowboy hats are playing in the beach shack we are sitting outside. I shit you not, they are doing a jaunty cover of Dylan's 'Blowin' in the Wind'. However, that's not actually the most surreal thing about this girls' holiday.

'Rosie, do you think there's enough gin in this?' my grandmother asks her older sister, my auntie Rose. 'It's so disappointing when you can't taste the gin properly. It's really not on.'

Nan and Rose are both wearing brightly coloured sarongs that look incongruous against their white hair, sensible sandals and Rose's walking stick.

'I think it's that local gin, Dot. It's just not the same. I'd ask for an extra measure if I were you,' Rose agrees. 'It's not very cold, either.'

'But we mustn't have ice, Rose!' Nan cries. 'Don't forget, Ells' – she looks at me sternly – 'don't *ever* have ice in your drink here.'

'I won't.' I take a gigantic slug of my Go-go Goa.

My auntie Ann and I exchange a glance. Ann is Nan and Rose's younger half-sister, so she's a youngster at seventy-two. She looks sophisticated with it, with her dark bob and sleek black swimsuit.

It's my first day of a 'girls' holiday' where I am the youngest by an average of forty-six years.

While it may be somewhat unusual at my age to be on holiday with three old ladies, I guess the idea of going on an exotic holiday to 'find myself' and 'discover my family history' is less so. In fact, I fear it may be pretty basic.

As I sit on the beach with a cocktail in my hand, I find myself thinking about how I got here. It's not exactly that I want to escape from my life – not any more. At this point, I think it's just that I need a break. A lot has happened and I've just been trying to get through it. Now I need to recalibrate.

I'm not sure where to start. I try to think back to my rock-bottom moment and, depressingly, more than one springs to mind. In the tradition of my own generation, I make a list – ticking them off in my mind like a BuzzFeed article.

You won't believe how this girl wrecked her life (#3 will blow your mind)!

- Stepmum dying/stepdad leaving – family falling apart, subsequent psychotic break; both parents now on third marriage.
- Breaking up with K after twelve years – breaking up a whole life, a whole fucking universe – for reasons that may have been . . . misguided?
- Immediate new boyfriend, me insisting 'it's not a rebound!' even after everyone had stopped listening, another traumatic break-up, more rebounds.
- Going into therapy after dating a potentially violent, certainly threatening, narcissist (the most pertinent point of which should be noted: I did not break up with him – *he ghosted me*).

Of course, it was a combination of all of these things. One long rock-bottom moment over the course of a few years.

I turned thirty feeling smugly ahead of the curve, with a long-term boyfriend, a charming flat by the sea, a lovely job, and a potential promising book deal on the horizon. I'd given up smoking; I baked a lot of cakes. But I also still went to Glastonbury every year and wore great eyeliner. My boyfriend was in a band and I wore vintage dresses and went shopping in markets on a Saturday for records and ironic knick-knacks. I was the kind of cool, sorted thirty-year-old that teenage-me would have dreamed of being. I don't know if I'm romanticizing in retrospect – it's easy to do, after all – but I know I was happy. I really liked my life, my friends, my family. Especially my family.

Since then, there's been death and divorce. There has been total and utter heartbreak that I wasn't sure I'd survive. If it were possible for grief to kill you, I would be dead. I smoke again. I can't remember the last time I made a cake, there's nobody to impress and I'd only eat the lot myself, so what's the point?

I was made redundant from my ideal job, then very unceremoniously sacked from the next one, for shagging my boss' ex-husband. I now have to commute from Brighton to London every day to try to keep a roof over my head. I live in a place I cannot afford and I'm in debt from having to buy out my ex in order to keep it. I don't sleep at night because I worry about the damp kitchen floor that I can't afford to have fixed. When people come over, I have to ask them not to stand by the back door in case they fall through the gaps in the rotten floorboards. To be fair, I also don't sleep at night because of Stupid Things I Said in 2004 (not to mention Clever Things I Should Have Said in 2009), so it's a fairly crowded field.

I've had a string of sort-of relationships that have seemed promising and then gone nowhere. Each time, with every month I get older, it chips away just a little bit more at my poor battle-scarred heart. I haven't had a dramatic break-up again – thank God, I genuinely don't think I could take it – but I haven't been in love for over two years now. I don't think the musician in LA who I met via Instagram and do sexy FaceTiming with really counts. Love was something I used to take for granted, and I don't have that luxury any more. Instead it's been a series of small-to-medium disappointments that have made me feel terrible about myself.

The crisis is over, but I don't feel better. I'm not completely in pieces any more, as I was a few years ago. I'm in therapy, which is helping a lot; there hasn't been a major drama in ages. But I'm tired. There is some pleasure in my life – mostly when I'm drinking wine with my mum or with my clever, funny girlfriends and laughing at the sad state of it all. However, there is a sense of deep, lasting joy that I feel is lacking – no children, work feeling less fulfilling, no meaningful love. I am the favourite person of nobody. Sounds self-pitying, but it's also true.

In fact, it's now that things have settled down and supposedly 'got better' that I've started feeling worst of all. When you're in the deep dark woods, fighting off wolves all over the place, you don't have room to think about what's happening. It's only after they've receded and you are, technically, safe that the silence seems suddenly deafening. I was left standing in the middle of the woods, as the sun came up and the wolves were a distant howling memory, going 'what the fuck just happened to me?'. Suddenly I had far too much space to think.

Now I'm here, on this crazy Indian beach – with wild dogs wandering around and cheesy dance music playing from the brightly decorated beach shacks, which all serve curry and lurid cocktails – I realize I'm happy to have a break from real life. My so-called strong independent life, where I live alone and go out a lot and have great friends. For some time now, I've felt like I am in the world very lightly – like I could disappear at any moment. I feel untethered, which should be exciting and freeing – but it's not. I pretend I'm fine, but I'm not. Something – maybe more than one thing, I don't even know – is missing.

If I'm honest, the silence *is* deafening. It's everywhere. It's in my kitchen while I scroll listlessly through Tinder, swiping left without really even looking, and drinking a bottle of red wine by myself without noticing until I realize that staggering to bed is harder than I thought. It's on the train in the morning, with the silent commuters who never make eye contact, while I pretend to sleep or sometimes cry silently without being sure why behind my sunglasses. It's definitely in bed at night, where I'm still not used to being alone, even after so long; I keep trying to learn to love it, to sleep starfished just because I can, but it doesn't work. I still sleep motionless, scrunched on one mean sliver of my luxurious king-size mattress. It's in my noisy workplace, where everyone wears headphones. It's even in the pub after work, where I go most evenings with a grumpy, reticent university lecturer who is not my boyfriend and who I'm not even sure likes me very much. Since arriving in India approximately six hours ago, I've already texted him repeatedly and not heard anything back. He's the latest in a line that is long-ish and getting longer.

I've lost sight of what constitutes a rock-bottom moment. Strolling into the reception of a Travelodge in my underwear to ask if they had a corkscrew because 'I thought it would be funny' (oh, and I was on a lot of cocaine at the time) was probably not my finest moment. But it wasn't rock-bottom. Standing outside the closed door of my own spare room, quietly asking 'Would you like a peppermint tea, maybe?' – because the man in there 'needed to be alone', because he was feeling 'aggressive' towards me – was scary. Still not rock-bottom. Falling over drunk in front of everyone at my dear friend Emma's wedding wasn't great. Crying on late-night trains on the way home has just become normal, to be honest. It's all been very kind of rock-not-quite-bottom.

Sitting here on the beach, it seems far enough away to give it a bit of thought now. Here in the sunshine with my nan and my aunties, with a long holiday stretching out before me, I feel like this might be a chance to finally get some perspective on it all.

So, if I had to pick one, like the one record you get to save on *Desert Island Discs*, I guess I do know the moment when it all began to fall apart.

January 2013

It is a freezing Monday morning and I have a dread feeling in my stomach. It follows me like a shadow or one of those horrible 'hangxiety' hangovers when you're not sure where your phone is, but you have a half-drunk bottle of wine in your handbag and eyeliner on your chin.

It won't go away and I have no idea why. I had a quiet weekend. I did some writing and I hung out with my boyfriend K. We went record shopping. I made a shepherd's pie. He went out to band practice and I pottered about in our flat. When he got home we watched a rubbish horror film. We have been together for approximately a decade. We like the same things. We have a shorthand.

The only unusual thing is that I haven't spoken to my mum and/or stepdad. I usually talk to at least one of them every day, sometimes multiple times. I tried to ring the house over the weekend, but there was no answer.

In the morning, I try to call again. The line rings and rings and rings. Only when I have pretty much given up does my mother answer. She sounds terrible.

'Mum, are you OK?'

'Not really. I've got this stupid flu and Stepdad's had to go to California for work. I'm a bit miffed about it, actually.'

I don't know why, it just doesn't sound quite right. I have never heard her use the word *miffed* before. It doesn't sound like something she would say. And Stepdad does go to California for work a lot, but it sounds a bit odd at such short notice, over a weekend.

I hang up the phone feeling like I've had a conversation with a cyborg that sounds a bit like a bunged-up version of my mother. My heroic mother who, it will turn out, didn't want to ruin an important day for me.

I'm not going to work at my day job today because my agent and I are going to see editors who are interested in a novel I have written. We have been working towards this for a long time. She's also taking me out for lunch, which is extra exciting, mostly because I really like saying things like 'Oh, sorry, I can't on Monday, my agent is taking me out for lunch'.

It's a big week, in fact. K and I are moving on Friday – from the tiny top-floor flat that we call 'The Garret' into an actual house. It has a spare bedroom and a garden. This is less for reasons of sensible grown-up-ness, more due to our still-idealistic dreams of the artistic bohemian life. We will have space for K to have a music studio and for me to write. That tiny terraced house will probably have a blue plaque outside it one day. We will be exactly like Ted Hughes and Sylvia Plath, but also totally the opposite of them. Life will be dreamy. We might get a dog. Or at least a cat.

So, I put on a vintage dress and head into London and smile my way through the day of meetings. Afterwards, I have planned to go out for dinner in Soho with my friend Alice, who is great fun. I've been looking forward to it for weeks.

With promises from editors that they'll be in touch, I say goodbye to my agent and walk towards Soho. I have time to kill so I try to call my stepdad. There is no answer, which is somehow unsurprising. What is surprising is that I get a UK ringtone. Not the weird long beeping-instead-of-ringing I'd hear if he were in California. Not only that, his work voicemail – which he maintains scrupulously with his whereabouts at all times – does not mention anything about being away.

I immediately call my mother. No answer. I keep calling until she picks up, which she does eventually. She sounds even worse than she did earlier.

'Mum, what's going on?'

'Nothing.'

'What's going on?'

'I don't know what you're talking about.'

'Please tell me.'

'But . . . but I don't want to.'

That's when the bottom drops out of my stomach. Or world. I don't even know.

'Please, Mum. It's OK. Just tell me.'

'Are you sitting down? Where are you?'

'Yes, I'm sitting down. I'm about to meet my friend Alice.'

I'm walking up and down Brewer Street and I can't feel my legs.

'I'm only telling you if you promise not to come here. I don't want you to worry about me.'

'OK . . .'

'Stepdad's left. He's met someone else.'

She went to Waitrose on Saturday morning and life was still normal. She got home an hour later and he had packed up half the house into the back of his car. She was still standing in the hallway when he drove off and life as we knew it was over.

Stepdad has brought me up since the age of eleven. He and my mum have been together for over twenty years. Their wedding was in the top-five happiest days of my life, maybe even top-three. He taught me to drive. He helped me with my maths homework. He introduced me to Alfred Hitchcock films, and to doomy Eighties goth music like Joy Division and The Cure. He is my skiing and cycling partner and basically my favourite person to hang out with. He always refers to me as his daughter and we would both fight anyone who dared to question the logistics of this.

My mum is beautiful and wonderful, the most fun and generous person I know. She and I are very close but if anything, sometimes we are too similar; he is the buffer that makes our family work. If my mum is the person I love the most in the world, he is the one I idolise. He and I are best friends, always have been; my mum would jokingly accuse us of ganging up on her, and I secretly enjoyed it.

It's not like I needed a dad when he came along – I have a dad and he's lovely. But my stepdad and I had a relationship outside of that – he was always a reliable and loving parent to me, but also we had loads in common and just got on really well. I suppose because he was slightly outside of being my actual parent, I found him easier to talk to and he came along at an age when I really needed that.

'I shouldn't have told you,' my mum says. 'I'm hoping he'll change his mind and I won't have to tell anyone. It'll be fine. I'm glad you're with your friend, you need someone to look after you.'

Have I mentioned my mum is a fucking hero? I'm still repeatedly telling her I love her when she hangs up the phone. I keep saying it, even after the line has gone dead.

I walk to Café Boheme very slowly, like my bones are made of glass. I'm early but I don't know where else to go. I don't cry, I don't react. I feel nothing. I guess the pins and needles numbness might be what they call 'shock' but who knows or actually cares?

I need a fucking drink. I get a cosy table for two and ask the handsome French waiter for a massive glass of white wine. I then sit there for an hour and don't touch it. I sit very, very still and stare at the wall for an hour, while that full massive glass of wine gathers condensation in front of me.

Alice walks in wearing a faux fur coat, enormous heels and bright, bright lipstick. She is the most beautiful thing I have ever seen.

'Ells!'

She hugs me into a cloud of fake fur and I could collapse into her arms but I do not. It occurs to me this might be the last normal night I can have for a long time, maybe forever. I don't want to make this real.

'How did your book meetings go?'

'Great. Brilliant. I think someone might actually buy my book! We should hear soon . . .'

'Well, that definitely calls for champagne!'

We have a lovely evening. We eat French food and flirt with the waiter and chat about boys. We smoke cigarettes sitting out on the pavement like we are actually in Paris (and not just a French restaurant), snuggled together arm-in-arm against the cold, blankets over our knees. We drink two bottles of champagne, joyously.

As soon as I leave and Alice goes out of sight, my bones stiffen up with sadness. I'm not sure this night is real but I suspect it might be. I sit on the train home and stare dead ahead at the seat in front of me.

I drag myself home, up the flights of stairs to our third-floor garret, which is already half packed up for the big move on Friday. I'm not sure if I'm relieved or disappointed that K is out. Mostly relieved, I suppose.

I don't switch on the lights. That would make it real. I don't take off my coat. That would make it real. I sit down on the nasty rental flat carpet in our mostly empty bedroom. I call Stepdad. He answers this time.

'Ells . . . Hang on, the reception here is terrible. I'll call you back from a landline.'

The reception *where* is terrible? I don't even know where he is. My phone starts ringing and the screen flashes up 'number withheld' and the sight of that makes me truly wish I were dead.

He made me mixtapes and took me to Camden Market

for the first time. We would have horror film marathons just the two of us because my mum and my sister didn't like them. When I was older we would get drunk together and smoke cigars and do air drums to Aerosmith. He's not my real dad. If he's not married to my mum then what are we to each other?

That's when, for the first time, it really hits me. I start crying. I won't stop for about four months.

This should be an important, deep conversation – but nobody is talking. We are both crying so hard that neither of us can speak. We stay like that on the phone for, if not hours, what feels like it.

'I'm sorry,' he says eventually. 'I'm sorry. I'm so sorry.'

'It's OK,' I reply, even though I have no idea what that means.

'I love you,' he says. 'It's going to be OK.'

As he hangs up the phone and I wonder where he even is, I'm not sure if it will be.

K gets home at 2 a.m. to find me hunched in a corner in the dark, like the girl from *The Ring*. I still have my coat and my winter boots on. I refuse to go to bed, so we both lie down on the sitting room floor until it begins to get light.

At 6 a.m., the universe delivers another unexpected fuck-you. My dad calls me to tell me that my grandpa ('Parpie') has died. Despite K asking me not to, I get up and go to work, because what the fuck else am I supposed to do?

April 2003

When I first met K, I was twenty-two. I was low-level bulimic and used to cut myself. I also took quite a lot of drugs and didn't think any of these things were particularly unusual, because everyone I knew did at least some of them too. I lived in a shared house where we saw a ghost, and a boy we didn't know once pissed on the sofa. I went out clubbing wearing 1970s evening dresses and I spent every Sunday so hungover I wanted to kill myself.

You don't need me to go into detail about these years, as you can read similar stories in numerous 'my lost twenties' memoirs. You know the drill. However, I will say that my lost years were much worse than any of these, guaranteed. Those books always depress me because the writers' rock-bottom moments always sounds exactly like a normal Tuesday night for me in the early Noughties.

Anyway, amid all the sad shagging, cocaine and throwing up – when I was twenty-two, my cool older friend Lauren asked me to be in a band. I couldn't play anything but I looked like I should be in a band, which was apparently good enough. She said her boyfriend Richie could teach me to play bass. Easy.

One Saturday afternoon, we drove to an obscure music shop in High Wycombe, where Richie knew someone who could 'get us a good deal' on a bass guitar. That turned out to be K, who looked like the lovechild of Keith Moon and Kurt Cobain in a brown cardigan – he had a mop of black hair, vast green eyes, incredible cheekbones and a slight air of oddness about him that I instantly liked. We got chatting about music and he told me about his band. He sold me a Fender Squier jazz bass, sunburst finish, and I gave him my number.

I chose him in the same way that I had chosen most of my boyfriends up to this point: because he looked cool and was in a band. Thus far, this strategy had not worked out particularly well. I had been dumped a lot by boys who just wanted to 'focus on their music', or 'not be tied down'. I'd had a lot of casual on-and-off things with guys who had thought I was 'really cool', while I had been secretly hoping they might fall in love with me and maybe want to marry me. Spoiler alert: they never, ever did. I had never met a boyfriend's parents or been on a romantic minibreak.

Amazingly, with K, things turned out differently. He called me the next day and asked me if I wanted to go out on a proper date. He took me for a picnic by the river. It turned out that he had been to art college and wanted to illustrate children's books. He loved Sherlock Holmes and French films and obscure Japanese cartoons I had never heard of. He wasn't quite as cool as I thought; he was much, much nicer.

He was twenty-seven and he lived in a house by himself. He cooked me pasta and didn't like drugs. He was slightly disapproving of my friends. I gradually stopped going out so much. I gave up smoking. He made me realize that some of the things I thought were normal were not.

We went on holiday to Devon together and the following year we moved to Brighton. He was the first boyfriend I had ever loved who loved me. He told me he didn't ever want to get married and I said that was fine. At last, I had something that was real. I could let go of the misguided dream of wanting to marry cool unattainable boys. This was a great compromise. We could forget convention and have a life together that suited us.

We had interesting people round for dinner, and London friends coming to visit all the time. A graffiti artist friend once slept on our sofa for a year. I helped K write lyrics for his band, and he painted a portrait of me in a hotel room in Paris that my mum still has on the wall in her house. I sat at the kitchen table every night in our top-floor Brighton flat, and for the first time I wrote a whole novel.

We went on holidays with my parents. K played music and did a lot of painting and set up a pop-up art gallery – way before these things were known as 'pop-ups' – back when having a friend with an empty shop in the centre of Brighton you could use was a normal occurrence.

When Amy Winehouse was at her skinniest and most drug-addled, and for some reason in those days we all thought it was OK to gawp, Stepdad once said to me, 'Imagine, if you hadn't met K, that would be you. Only without the talent.' How we all laughed.

Then ten years later – on that freezing cold Monday in January – the world I thought I knew fell apart and K had to watch me regress before his eyes.

Turns out, it's acceptable(ish) to be a total fuck-up when you're twenty-two. At thirty-two, it's quite embarrassing. Especially when it's about something as prosaic as a parental divorce. I'd already been through one once, at the age of eleven, and handled it with a lot more grace as a child than I managed to do as an adult. The acute humiliation of this knowledge did not help.

I didn't know that stilted phone conversation on the floor of my rental flat would be the last conversation we would ever have. Stepdad never spoke to any of us again. He very quickly began to communicate solely through solicitors' letters. That was when I wrote him an email saying I didn't want to speak to him again, not that he'd tried particularly hard. When he told me that he loved me and it would be OK, I had no idea I would never hear his voice ever again. I might have tried to say more if I'd known that.

The only way I could get through this was by telling myself he had been kidnapped and someone – possibly Liam Neeson or Jason Statham – was holding a gun to his head and making him do these things against his will.

It's hard to explain how much I loved Stepdad and how

much it fucked me up to lose him. There is something profoundly unsettling about having the rug ripped out from under your feet just as you think you're living like a real adult and you've got everything under control for the first time in your life. I was so proud of myself for how far I'd come from that sad, bulimic, chain-smoking, falling-drunk-off-the-table twenty-two-year-old. Turns out she'd been waiting in the wings the whole time, through all those grown-up minibreaks on the Eurostar and trips to Ikea and all the other things I wrongly thought made me a functional adult.

But mostly, I was just unbearably sad because I loved him so much. My heart was broken in a way that it could never have been by a mere boyfriend. It was the worst break-up imaginable. It taught me that I'd been wrong during those years of painstakingly building up my self-esteem. You can't trust anyone. People will leave you and they will disappear. Love is not unconditional. You will not be enough. Ever. The person who I thought loved me the most, literally, disappeared.

I got very thin. I started smoking again. I got a huge tattoo and told myself it would stop me from cutting myself, a habit so old it was almost forgotten, but somehow crept back in, under the American Apparel thigh-high socks I started insisting on wearing to bed every night. Quite embarrassing in someone over thirty, really. I lived in fear of K or anybody else finding out. I hid razorblades in strange places. I took two scalding hot baths a day with the doors locked.

I cried constantly. Walking down the street, at work, in

bed every night. I didn't want to be touched because I would fall to pieces. I didn't want anyone to be kind to me.

I became obsessed with fake tan, a product I had only ever sneered at previously. My skin turned darker and darker, as it collected in my clavicles and between my fingers like nicotine stains. I think I just wanted to be in a different skin.

I stopped sleeping altogether. I was so manic, I kept having what I thought were brilliant ideas, which made no sense. I started writing a 'brilliant' new novel, and then when I read it back, it barely even contained real words.

Stranger and stranger superstitions started to take up more and more of my day. I once nearly choked in the house by myself, as I had taken to walking around with a piece of rose quartz in my mouth at all times. Just carrying it with me wasn't enough.

I started seeing cats everywhere I went, convinced it was 'a sign'. I started a spreadsheet of every cat I saw, with columns entitled 'location/colour/character/what they were trying to tell me'. The spreadsheet went so far as to include such entries as 'Thought I saw a cat under a seat on the train. Followed it. There was no cat'.

A couple of months passed and things did not get better. To the outside world, it didn't look so bad. I managed to go to work and even to see friends occasionally, but I was just trying to get through the days. Nobody realized quite how bad it was, but I had a force field around me that made other people nervous.

My sister and my nan seemed to get over the shock relatively quickly, but my mum and I did not. My mum kept telling me she was 'fine' but was very evidently not fine. I did the same thing back. Every time my phone rang, I braced myself for the news that my mother had committed suicide. I could not see a way that she or I would get out of this alive.

This was perhaps more understandable for my mum than for me. But I just couldn't get over it. Everything was ruined. Life felt not only futile but fucking impossible. I just couldn't seem to function like a normal human being. I could not stop crying. But I had K, which seemed to make people think I must be fine. He would look after me, just like he always had.

We started sleeping further apart. We stopped talking. Neither of us was capable of it. K tried to call Stepdad to tell him he thought I was going to kill myself. Stepdad didn't answer and never called him back.

I went to the doctor and received a letter saying I would be put on a waiting list for psychiatric assessment. A few weeks later I went for the assessment and received another letter saying I would be treated as priority and then nothing happened.

When it became apparent that Stepdad was not going to come back or start behaving like a decent human any time soon, my mum and I went to Hatton Garden to sell her jewellery, then went and spent some of our pirate spoils on a decadent lunch. The guy in the dodgy pawn shop liked us, gave us an extra £50 note from the wedge in his breast pocket, to buy a bottle of champagne on him. If nothing else, we always do our best to make bad times glamorous.

I am not as pragmatic as my mother, even though I could

do with the money. My prize possession was a Swiss Army watch that Stepdad gave me, that used to be his. I used to wear it every day, with inordinate pride. Either selling it or throwing it away seemed wrong, somehow. For weeks I kept it in my desk drawer at work, as I didn't want it in the house.

One morning, after drinking a lot of coffee, I had a flash of inspiration. I pissed on it and posted it to him in a Jiffy bag (to his work address, I still don't know where he lives) that developed a film of condensation on the inside before I'd even sealed it up. I guess it was the combination of fury, betrayal and shame that made this seem like a perfectly rational course of action. I told people about this calmly, like it was quite a normal thing to do.

Just over six months after Stepdad left, in July, we were supposed to be going on holiday. It had been booked in advance as a family occasion, to celebrate Stepdad's birthday and my mum's and his wedding anniversary. It was non-refundable, so we decided to go anyway. It was a very strange week.

My mum would say she was 'going for a walk' (aka disappearing down the beach to cry like her heart was broken, which was logical because it was), and everyone else would politely pretend not to notice, while I followed her even though she didn't want me to. So she and I ended up going for long walks every day, holding hands, in near silence. I couldn't tell her things like 'it's going to be OK' because that would be a lie, so mostly I just said 'yeah, I know, me too'. I'm not sure it helped.

My mum and I drank a litre of cheap white wine with our lunch each day and then kept going. K couldn't deal with it and took to bed for two days, refusing to talk to any of us. My poor sister and her boyfriend were left to try to jolly things up. I guess I shouldn't blame K – it was stressful for everyone – but I couldn't help thinking this wasn't exactly helpful of him.

K and I had already nearly broken up, only a year earlier. Another terrible crisis point – my stepmum Sue had died, suddenly, at the age of fifty-one. Like Stepdad, she had been in my life since I was eleven and had a huge hand in bringing me up. She was the most full-of-life woman I can picture, and she left behind two sons – both much younger than me – whom she adored fiercely. She shouldn't have died, that's all I can still think about it.

At Sue's funeral, I said 'I want to have a baby', the first time I had ever really had this thought, let alone spoken it out loud. It did not go away.

K did not react to this as I'd hoped. He simply refused to discuss it. This was not what we had agreed; as he saw it, I was reneging on our deal, which was to be non-conformist and not care about such things. I was letting the side down. He was furious with me. I was so sad and so shocked, I agreed to shut up and hope it would go away.

I can see what I was trying to do, although neither of us could at the time. I'd had a tricky, unsettled childhood but then things had calmed down – four parents, new stepbrothers on my dad's side, the classic Dad's-every-other-weekend routine. My life had hinged on that stability for so long that

I thought I could count on it. Now I had lost so much of that, no wonder I was desperate for change, to make a brand new life for us that looked different, instead of hanging around in the ruins.

After we came back from our disastrous holiday, more months went by and I began to resemble a normal human again. I became less frail. I stopped dyeing myself orange. I slept better at night and sometimes I could go a day without crying. After a while, it looked to the naked eye like the crisis had passed. K seemed mostly relieved that we'd got through it without him having to talk about it.

So, we'd made it through. Life was a bit worse and we were a bit different, but we seemed to have come out the other side together. Sort of.

Things began to look brighter when I started pouring my energy into writing. This was how I would save myself, I decided. Once I got going, the words flooded out of me with an unstoppable intensity.

I wrote a whole novel in six weeks straight, barely sleeping, not wanting to do anything else. Running away from my own life. I wrote it mostly in bed, just to stay warm – the new house had turned into a disaster.

It was freezing cold, damp and full of woodlice, and it turned out that all the floors were rotten. Everything was falling apart around us.

So, while my life was quietly in ruins, I escaped from it all by writing a sweet romantic comedy for teenagers. And – after years of trying, with various small degrees of success – somehow it ended up being the best thing I had ever written.

Suddenly life got exciting again. My agent texted me while I was at work to tell me a big publisher wanted to buy the book I had written.

I immediately rang K and my mum to tell them the news. Even as I was saying it, it didn't feel real. My mum cried with joy for me, and K took me out for cocktails that night to celebrate.

It was exactly then that all of the stress started coming out in weird physical ways. The next morning (now that I supposedly had everything I had ever wanted in my whole life) I woke up with such intense pins and needles down my right-hand side, I could barely use that side of my body. I had to call a cab to take me to work, as I couldn't manage the twenty-minute walk. I had recently started a new job for a small healthcare publisher, so I struggled through the day trying to make sure nobody noticed. This was supposed to be the best time of my life! Yes, I was so excited! No, I couldn't believe it either!

I began to have multiple ocular migraines every day, so severe and constant that I stopped driving, out of pure fear. I haven't driven since and now I've forgotten how. More weird symptoms seemed to develop every day. I started throwing up for no reason, having to spend hours hiding in the loo at work because I was incapable of functioning like a normal human in public. Just like when I used to be bulimic, how retro!

I took to spending my evenings lying in a darkened room, unable to move. I became convinced I was probably dying. I was sent for blood tests and MRIs, and nobody could find anything wrong with me. I concluded that I was definitely dying.

A kind neurologist poked me with needles, and told me to come off the Pill immediately. I was put on it when I was seventeen because I had a burst ovarian cyst, and the Pill reduces the risk of recurrence. I don't think anybody ever asked me if I suffered from migraines, which I always have. The neurologist was appalled that I was on the Pill at all – let alone that I had solidly been on it for fifteen years. She said my stroke risk, what with the migraines and the smoking – oh, and the family history of strokes – was probably through the roof.

I came off the Pill and immediately felt better. When I told K this, he gave me a funny look I had never seen before and asked me if I didn't think this was 'a bit too convenient'. I was so shocked, I didn't know what he meant at first. Then it turned into a horrible argument.

'It's not exactly a surprise.' He shrugged. 'We've been together over ten years. This is what happens to everyone in the end, isn't it? Girls pretend they're cool and they want the same things as you, then next thing you know they've trapped you into getting married and having *offspring* and you have to pretend to be happy about it or everyone thinks it's you who's the bastard.'

I asked him if he really felt like we were on opposing sides now, and he said he wasn't sure. That was the beginning of the end.

We limped on, sadly and undramatically, for a few months. We went on holiday to Hydra, a tiny island where Leonard Cohen used to live and wrote many of his most famous songs – and was therefore my dream destination. I sat on our lovely roof terrace, drinking wine, while K slept a lot. I went for a lot of long walks by myself. We were polite to each other. We both did our best and it wasn't quite good enough.

Then – almost inevitably, something had to happen – I met a man through work: a funny and handsome journalist. While I had a boyfriend at home who was barely speaking to me, I started saying I was going out with 'colleagues' and instead going to grown-up jazz nights with The Journalist, where we would drink red wine and talk about how our partners 'didn't understand us'.

I convinced myself it was OK, because we hadn't actually slept together. But I'm not that naive – I know hanging around in bars and bitching about how useless your boyfriend is . . . well, it's not cool. In fact, it is not only uncool, but incredibly dangerous.

The ending finally happened on a perfectly normal week-night. K and I went round to our neighbours' house for dinner. They had recently had twins; we all drank wine and ate takeaway fish and chips while the babies slept – one of them on me, while I happily ate my dinner one-handed. If I were allowed to be honest, I would admit this is actually what I would like my own life to look like. As far as I was concerned, it was a lovely evening.

We got home and closed the front door. I was still taking off my coat when I realized that K was just standing there and staring at me.

'This isn't going to work,' he said. 'That's what you want, isn't it? All of that. I would rather fucking hang myself. We're going to have to break up.'

I burst into tears and said yes, I agreed. He burst into tears and said he didn't really mean it. It was too late. It was the end.

Well, except it wasn't. Because we were grown-ups who co-owned a house and a lot of shared furniture. We still had to go on a trip to New York for my sister's thirtieth birthday, which was like slow torture. Then we had to live in the house together for four months while we argued over what to do with it. Eventually I borrowed money to buy him out.

My family – what remained of it – were devastated. Our friends had to awkwardly pick sides. It was like getting divorced without the legitimacy of having been married. We had built a whole life together, but saying 'my boyfriend and I are breaking up' sounded so teenage and inconsequential.

When K and I broke up, I felt desperate for more. More forward motion in life. More passion. More excitement. Something finally happening, not just hanging around waiting for everyone to die or disappear in the end.

I spend the next five years of my life wondering how the fuck I ended up with so much less.

December 2014

While K is finally moving out, I can't bear to be around for it. So I escape to New York with my mum.

My mum and I are soulmates, very close and scarily similar. If you look at old pictures of us at the same ages, sometimes it's hard to tell which of us it is. It freaks us both out. Now I'm an adult, we are more like naughty sisters who drink wine and have kitchen discos together.

She travels to New York a lot for work and has a lot of friends in the city. We decide this would be the ideal place for a change of scene, and spend money that neither of us can afford on the trip. We get so drunk and overexcited on the flight out that a stewardess has to ask us to be quiet. We are also asked whether there has been a death in the family when we both weep loudly while watching *Beaches*.

Unfortunately, just as we arrive, so does a major snow-storm. It's a freakish cold snap even for the freezing New York winter. There are weather warnings in place and people are advised not to go outdoors.

Of course, my mum and I decide to ignore this advice. We are on holiday, after all! We get wrapped up and go out for a walk in Central Park. It's so cold, the ice rink is closed. There is not another human to be seen. It's apocalyptic.

It's so foggy we have to hold hands to keep together, and before long of course we realize that we are horribly lost. It's funny at first, but then we realize we can't feel our faces and become convinced that this is how we are going to die. When the snow thaws, they will find us and, worst of all, they will say how stupid we were to have ignored all those weather warnings.

When we eventually find our way out of the park, there are no cabs because everyone is indoors, so we have to walk sixteen blocks back to our hotel. When we arrive back there, the concierge brings us brandy and blankets.

After that, we decide not to go outdoors again. We do not leave the hotel for the rest of our holiday, not once. It's strangely relaxing. We order room service. We sit up in our twin beds like Bert and Ernie, and watch TV. We take it in turns to have long hot baths. I go up to the hotel gym and run for hours on the treadmill, looking out of the panoramic windows at nothing but falling snow. We go down to the bar for cocktails and then go straight back up to bed. We soon feel happily institutionalized, like we have always been there and might never leave.

The thing we enjoy the most, and do more than once, is to both get into my bed and watch *Grey Gardens* on my laptop.

My mum and I have long been obsessive fans of the film

Grey Gardens, but on this trip, our love for it reaches new heights. Watching it together here feels very fitting. It's a strange 1970s documentary about an aristocratic but eccentric and broke mother and daughter, 'Big Edie' and 'Little Edie', who live together in their dilapidated mansion, Grey Gardens, with a lot of cats and a few raccoons.

They love each other fiercely but they bicker a lot. They wear threadbare old fur coats and diamond necklaces while singing show tunes and drinking cocktails out of jam jars. They are magnificent.

We put on lipstick and headscarves with our hotel bathrobes, crack open the overpriced minibar wine and watch it again and again. We quote it at each other a lot and take to addressing each other in exaggerated New England aristolady accents.

'Could you simply be a darling and pass me the wine please, Little Edie?'

'Of course, Mother darling. I do like your headscarf.'

'Why, thank you. It was given to me by my cousin Jackie Kennedy. I'm simply mad about it!'

Not long after we get back, I get a tattoo on my wrist that reads 'staunch'. This comes from my favourite scene in *Grey Gardens*, in which Little Edie rants about the various relatives who have underestimated her, before realizing that she is, in fact, 'a staunch woman' and therefore not to be messed with. 'And let me tell you, there is nothing worse than a staunch woman' – because 'they don't weaken, no matter what'.

My secret long-held dream is for my mum, my nan and I

to one day live together in *Grey Gardens*-style drunken squalor, bickering and singing and drinking cocktails in bed out of old jam jars.

I am trying very hard to be staunch. My mum is staunch. She has been through a lot and always done it with a tremendous amount of style. We are both trying our best.

January 2015

And then I get home to an empty house and suddenly I am living entirely on my own for the first time in my life. I am extremely aware that I have gone from being ahead of the curve to way behind it. A story like this should really involve a hedonistic and secretly oh-so traumatic blur of drinking, drugs and shagging in my twenties, followed by a revelation and meeting a 'nice' man to settle down with in my early thirties. That's the correct narrative, right?

Except somehow I am now thirty-four and everything has gone wrong. In the interim, most of my close friends have 'settled down' (terrible phrase; if I ever 'settle down' please fucking shoot me). They are now in the place I was at during my early twenties – excited about making Sunday roasts for gangs of cool friends, talking about paint colours and the best place to buy a green velvet sofa as seen on everybody's Instagram, whereas I am now the only single one. And they're doing it more proficiently than I did, because they all seem to be planning weddings and talking about maybe coming off the Pill.

I suddenly feel very old and very out of step with other people of my age. Most of them have never had a relationship as long as mine with K, and don't understand what it's like to have been through a break-up that huge. People say 'well, at least you didn't have kids' as if that must make it really easy. Frankly, I wish more than anything that I had a baby to show for it, at least. When my mum was my age, she had a twelve-year-old and a nine-year-old – the comparison is so depressing.

I feel battle-scarred and ancient, but my life is less 'grown-up' and more unsettled than it has ever been. If I were younger, I guess I'd spend this time going out every night and having one-night stands, but that's not really an option at this point. I work long hours in my new day job for a science publisher (having been sacked from the last one, due to The Journalist unfortunately being my boss's ex-husband), and I now have a long commute, so I leave the house every morning before 7 a.m. and get home after 7 p.m. In the evenings, I either eat a vast trough of pasta for dinner and go straight to bed, or I sit at my kitchen table listening to music and scrolling through Tinder while smoking roll-ups and drinking a whole bottle of red wine by myself.

I love hanging out with my girlfriends, but by our age that usually means drinking wine around somebody's kitchen table, which is great but means I am unlikely ever to meet anybody new. They all seem so much more content with life than I am.

It's my job to be the cheerful one who doesn't give a fuck;

if I can't live up to that, I'm not sure who to be. I try to talk to one friend about how I'm feeling – old, exhausted, insecure, pointlessly angry about all that wasted time, pretty much hopeless – and I guess it makes her feel uncomfortable, because she shuts it down pretty quickly by saying this is 'not very feminist' of me.

Once or twice a week, I go out for lunch or drinks with The Lecturer. The Lecturer is a confusing presence in my life. We met through distant friends, on one of those random Thursday evenings when going to someone's birthday drinks seems marginally better than getting on the train home.

On first sight, I was not remotely interested in him. He wasn't my type and I imagined we had nothing whatsoever in common. I assumed he must be boring, despite his too-long Nineties grunge hair – which I strongly suspected might be more by accident than design. He seemed utterly unenthused and bitched about everyone all evening, so I wasn't expecting it when he looked me up on Facebook late that same night. I only replied because I was a bit bored and drunk on the way home.

He claims to hate all humans and have no social skills, yet he takes to sending me long emails (which admittedly make me laugh) and texting me most days. I bother to reply about a third of the time, and yet still he perseveres. Eventually, I end up hanging out with him because I have nothing much else to do. The university where he works is around the corner from my office, so maybe he's just bored too.

He takes me out for pink cocktails on a rooftop bar, and

I turn up with dirty hair and a hangover. I have a surprising amount of fun and agree to go for drinks again. 'Soon', at his insistence.

On our nights out together we stay out drinking and talking for so long that I sometimes miss the last train home and have to stay the night with other friends because The Lecturer won't let me come back to his flat with him. We sneak out for lunches together in the pub and have such a nice time we agree to meet again in the same pub three hours later.

I become increasingly intrigued by him, with his corduroy jackets and his air of ennui. Sometimes I gaze at him and think, actually, maybe he is a bit like Ted Hughes or Heathcliff.

I'm dating all sorts of other unsuitable people, but nothing seems to stick. I'm not sure how I feel about The Lecturer, but I grudgingly have to admit that he is clever and interesting, and his texts always cheer me up. He becomes a constant backdrop. I start measuring my Tinder matches by whether they are as smart and funny as The Lecturer. It begins to dawn on me that most of them don't get me in the way that he does, so I start hanging out with him in the pub more and more.

Besides, it beats drinking by myself at the kitchen table, which I also seem to spend more and more of my time doing. While I sink a bottle of red wine and chain-smoke, sometimes I dance around to Patti Smith and feel free and feminist and vindicated, and sometimes I listen to Joni Mitchell and cry my eyes out.

My most pressing concerns, as evidenced by my late-night Google search history:

> coolest tattoo shop east london
> cheap botox clinic
> basic north korea politics explanation
> best instagram filter
> how old is cole sprouse
> full moon cleanse for crystal dildo
> health risks smoking over 30
> smear test eroded cervix
> mexican kitchen tiles

This seems to sum up the strange hinterland I find myself inhabiting. The constant low-level feeling that I'm running out of time causes me to make strange, panicked decisions. I know I'm looking for something but I'm not sure what it is, so I keep trying to make everything into that thing.

Unsuitable guys from Tinder. Internet stalking and unsolicited Instagram messages to boys I dated when I was twenty-one. The Lecturer. I keep hoping I can magically turn them into *it*, the thing that I am looking for. But I can't.

January 2015

I feel very alone. On paper, I have so many friends, this is almost embarrassing to admit. But I don't feel like I have many people I can talk to these days. Nobody gets it, so I just say I'm fine. I guess this blatant lying alienates people, because old friends seem a bit annoyed with me and new friends all think I'm someone I'm not, which makes me feel even lonelier.

There's not really anywhere else to turn. Although I am close to both of my parents, they have never been the types to make their children the centre of the universe, which mostly I'm pretty sure has been good for us. They simply don't have the time; they've got their own dramas. Having been recently bereaved and deserted, respectively, both of them are soon embroiled in various dating sagas and have more than enough going on in their own lives.

I'm the eldest, and I can't dump my own stress onto my little sister. That's not how the world is supposed to work (although my 'little' sister Katy has in fact always been The

Sensible One). She was less close with both of my stepparents than I was and, conversely, she is thriving. It's the one uncomplicatedly good thing happening in our family. She suddenly gets serious and moves in with her boyfriend, whom she has known since we were at school and we all adore. She doesn't need me bringing her down.

And so, maybe surprisingly, the person I end up talking to the most about everything that's going on in my life is my grandmother.

My nan and I have always been close. My parents both worked and she lived nearby, so every day my sister and I would go to her house after school. She would make us cheese on toast while we did our homework and watched *Neighbours*, until my mum came and picked us up to go home for dinner. At the time, I sometimes used to be a bit embarrassed and resentful that I had to be different from the other girls at school, who all got collected by their mums in sporty hatchbacks, but now of course I only remember it as very cosy and idyllic.

So I'm lucky to have always had that sort of close, everyday relationship with a grandparent, and I know I'm extremely lucky at my age still to have a living grandmother (I even had a great-grandmother until I was twenty-one). Since I've grown up and left home, she and I have always seen a lot of each other and spoken on the phone most days.

When I find myself living alone for the first time, I speak to her more and more. This is often because, being retired and also living alone, she is the one most likely to answer the phone.

She is warm and generous and patient with me, like a grandmother off the telly, but she is also sometimes very tactless, which makes me love her all the more and reminds me she's just a person like me, not a wise elder-woman of the tribe at all times.

'This must be especially hard for you,' she said after my stepdad left, 'because you really thought he loved you the most and that turned out not to be true.'

She's also funny, always entertaining and unfailingly, inspirationally, optimistic. She also often tells me 'not to worry about things so much' and 'look for the silver lining' and banal shit like that, which would annoy me massively if not for the fact that she has lived a lot longer than I have, so I should probably just shut up and listen. Failing all else, she often bursts into 'inspirational' song: 'Smile, though your heart is breaking . . .', 'You are my sunshine . . .'. That sort of thing.

She is sympathetic to my current situation, but she is also taken aback, mostly by the level of time and effort I put into feeling all these feelings. She didn't have time for that sort of thing when she was my age. She was too busy working a full-time job, maintaining a flat, bringing up two children as a single mother, helping to look after her parents and siblings, carrying groceries home on the bus and not having enough money to buy a new skirt.

My grandmother is definitely staunch. I currently fear I am not. I am certainly not country strong; I am city weak. Compared to my grandmother, or my mother, at my age – I feel like a baby. A pathetic baby who smokes and drinks too much.

My nan, however, is unequivocally staunch. She's a woman who's had a lot of reason to feel sorry for herself in her life, but she never, ever does. Also she calls hairspray 'lacquer' and blusher 'rouge', like a true Edie would. Also like the Edies, she is what you might call 'a character'.

Nan has more friends than anybody else I have ever met in my entire life. My sister Katy and I are always being dragged 'for coffee' to meet some random friend of hers. It usually transpires that she met them on the bus. She meets everybody on the bus. Sometimes she knows them from Spanish class, or singing club, or because they're Maureen's friend, or you know Stella down the road whose son works for M&S, and after that I stop listening. Sometimes she knows them from church. She's deeply religious, but somehow it's not annoying – weirdly, I find it sort of comforting when she says 'God bless you' to me before she hangs up the phone every time, and tells me frequently that she prays for me, ('and K' as she continues to tack on for quite some time). My sister and I used to be obsessed with her friend from church who was a porn star, who became a born-again. That was fun.

When I was little, many of my favourite activities used to involve Nan (or Dorothea, or Dot, as she is more commonly known):

- Spending hours trawling through her old jewellery box, which played *Isle of Capri*, and telling her which pieces I would like her to leave me 'when she died' (mostly the charm bracelet and the opal ring, please).

- Sniffing her lipstick, which was powdery and smelled floral, like Nan lipstick always, always does.
- Stroking the loose skin on her inner arm, which would make me sleepy, and then making her sing me 'Golden Slumbers' again and again until I fell asleep.
- Begging her to let me light one of her very special Christmas candles, then crying hysterically when it melted.
- Being allowed to suck the lemon out of her gin and tonic.

My nan's life has been extraordinary. She was born and brought up in India, a fourth-generation immigrant under the deeply problematic British Raj. Partition, which left over a million people dead and countless others displaced (the largest forced migration of people in history that wasn't due to war or famine), happened when she was sixteen.

She came to the UK and trained as a nurse, worked in community health, and was a single mum in the Sixties when that was really not the done thing. She has spent her life being self-sufficient, worked really hard for everything she's ever had, and was generally a bit of a girl-boss way before that term was ever invented.

Which is why, when I become single and find myself living alone for the first time in my adult life, she is the logical person to talk to. If I'm at home, most evenings I talk on the phone for an hour or so to my nan. We are in surprisingly similar life situations considering there is almost exactly fifty years between us.

Often I'll call her after we've both listened to *The Archers*. I'll have a red wine, she'll have a sherry. Nan has a glass of sherry and some Hula Hoops (or sometimes Mini Cheddars) in a fancy bowl every evening before dinner. I still think this is impossibly chic and I have tried valiantly to do the same, only I always end up drinking the whole bottle without noticing and by then I can't be bothered to cook so the Hula Hoops end up being my dinner and I have a dreadful hangover in the morning.

Anyway, while we chat on the phone of an evening, she'll be half-watching *Coronation Street*; I will not be. We will discuss what we're both going to have for dinner. We are often both having some permutation of eggs. She'll tell me about her Spanish homework and singing club and who she went out for lunch with that day. I'll tell her about writing and my friends' love lives ('How's Alice getting on? What about Em and Pete?') and complain about whoever it is I'm sleeping with and not-really going out with.

'These men today don't know their arse from their elbow if you ask me,' she'll say, in her posh nan voice.

It's often the highlight of my day.

Present Day

I have a very, very strong feeling of 'what the actual fuck have I done?'. I am still hungover from drinking White Russians round at Natalie's on New Year's Eve. It's 5:30 a.m. It's raining, heavily. When I get on the Gatwick Express, it's too early even to be able to get a coffee at the station.

I tell myself I have this feeling before every big trip I've ever done, and in the end I'm always glad I did it. Before I spent my twenty-ninth birthday by myself at the Chelsea Hotel in New York, I cried in the cab to Heathrow, wishing I could just stay at home and watch telly instead (but of course that trip turned out to be life-affirming and wonderful). I spent the whole flight to Marrakech quietly hoping not to be murdered, and then it ended up being my favourite city in the world. I tell myself I always feel suddenly and unexpectedly anxious and weepy just before a trip, and it's always worse when it's a trip by myself.

This is even more daunting than a trip by myself. It's a trip on which I will be responsible for two quite high-maintenance octogenarians, in the manner of an old-fashioned lady's companion from a Daphne du Maurier novel or similar. Partly because they need the help with travelling, and I think partly because they feel sorry for me because my sister is getting married, I have ended up being the chosen grandchild to come with them on this momentous trip back to India.

So, for the coming weeks I'm going to be travelling around India with my grandmother, her older sister Rose and their younger half-sister Ann. It occurs to me that to have agreed to this, I may have gone more mad that I did that time I thought cats were talking to me.

We have decided on Goa, which was chosen mostly for practical rather than sentimental reasons. Nan and Rose need a comfortable resort that makes life as easy for them as possible, and this was the best we could find. They are not up for a bustling city, and where they went to school is in the mountains, now over the border in Pakistan, and Nan isn't sure she can manage the journey this would involve.

Apparently there is some Portuguese blood on one side of the family and Ann's grandmother may have been from Goa. While we're there we want to have an ask-around about the name Baptiste and the connection to our family. However, Baptiste turns out to be a common name in Goa.

Although we are not going to see the places where they lived, we still feel that this is a family pilgrimage. We're going back to the country where my grandmother and aunts were all born, so that we can eat the food, speak the language and tell family stories.

I would really like to go and see the places where they grew up and lived, but for now this is a good toe in the water for me. Nan keeps reminding me that it will be a culture shock; it has long been a trope that I may not be able to 'cope' with some aspects of India. Goa is the gentle option, and – for various reasons – we all need a little bit of gentleness.

Before any of that, we have an airport and a long-haul flight to get through.

I have a rucksack on my back and I'm pulling my small wheelie suitcase behind me. I've come dressed for long-haul travel – i.e. looking like total, utter shit. I am wearing an old baggy T-shirt that says 'More issues than *Vogue*' on it, plus several thousand layers of deeply unattractive cardigans and hoodies.

I am, as instructed, meeting my nan at the taxi drop-off area so I can carry her bags for her. We are approximately two hours earlier than we need to be, on top of a flight time that was already very bloody early, but I knew better than to try and debate about this. I am very excited about running off and skipping January in favour of a proper adventure, but I am also very tired and grumpy and I am being rained on.

My nan is escorted out of her cab by a driver with an umbrella. She is wearing pearls.

'Darling! Everyone has *issues* these days, don't they?' she says by way of greeting as she hugs me, looking slightly disapprovingly at my T-shirt. 'I'm so excited, aren't you?'

Andy Warhol said you should point out your own flaws before someone else does. I like to think I'm being self-aware and ironic. But suddenly from my nan's point of view I can see how this would look sort of . . . odd. Like, why would you choose to advertise that you have 'issues'? It's not something to be particularly proud of, or to joke about.

Fortunately, I don't have long to contemplate this, because my nan appears to have brought three hand luggage bags ('but one's my handbag, darling') and the biggest suitcase I have ever seen.

'What have you got in here?' I ask through gritted teeth as I wonder if we'll have to pay excess baggage charges.

'It's mostly my medication,' she tells me. 'You know, when you get to my age, darling . . .'

One of the bags appears to have nothing but books and a cushion in it, but obviously I can't argue. Well played, Nan.

We find our fellow travellers, Auntie Rose and Auntie Ann, get rained on a lot, discover that the travelator thing to get into the terminal is broken, struggle with lifts and then there's some technical problem with checking in that results in a long queue and having to carry the bags to another check-in desk on the other side of the airport.

I realize complaining about any of this sounds spoiled, but I feel responsible for making sure this goes smoothly and everyone is OK, which is making me anxious – mostly because I'm not sure I'm capable of it.

'Careful with that trolley, Ells,' appears to have become the mantra.

We're finally getting to the front of the queue when a young couple, a girl and a boy with huge backpacks, push in front of us. They're chatting excitedly and don't even seem to have noticed we are standing right there. I'm prepared to just let it go.

'Excuse me,' Rose says politely.

They either don't hear her or continue to ignore her.

'Excuse me!' she says more loudly this time.

The boy turns around, looking slightly annoyed. The girl continues to ignore Rose's existence.

'You pushed in front of us,' Rose explains to him, quite patiently. 'We are in this queue and you pushed right in front of us.'

'I didn't see you,' he says defensively, not apologising.

'That's the problem, you see. I'm completely invisible to you because I'm old.'

She says it with a smile, just stating a fact. The young man doesn't say anything else, or even try to apologise – I think it's because he's too embarrassed. His girlfriend still hasn't acknowledged our existence. They scuttle behind us as we go to the front. Rose winks at me.

I am extremely conscious that airports must be especially hard work when you're in your eighties – most things are; if I've learned one thing from these ladies it's that you have to be hard as nails to get old – but they get to have wheelchairs.

'The power of mobility and invisibility, it seems,' Rose notes sagely.

Neither Nan nor Rose is a wheelchair user in day-to-day life, but it turns out anyone can ask for 'special assistance' on a plane. They'll take you from check-in to your gate and onto the plane, which otherwise involves a lot of schlepping. I feel a bit embarrassed as the young, able-bodied tagalong. However, I'm pleased to report I got over it when we were ushered through the extra-quick security queue like it was Studio 54.

We make it onto the plane with only one minor argument, and that's the same argument my nan and I have whenever I stay at her house for the weekend.

'Darling, nip to the shop and get a paper for me, will you?'

'No. When you say "paper" I know what you mean. I'll get you a *Guardian* if you like.'

'The *Guardian*! Stop being ridiculous. Just go to the shop. I'll give you the money.'

'Nan, the *Daily Mail* is a Nazi rag. I'm not doing it.'

'You know I only get it for the crossword. Puzzles are supposed to stave off dementia, you know. Just go to the shop for me. I so rarely ask you to do anything.'

'Fine.'

I always – always – end up buying my nan a *Daily Mail*. I am always utterly baffled by this. She worked in the public sector all of her life and is evangelical about the NHS, yet she cannot bring herself ever to consider 'leftie' activities such as reading the *Guardian* or voting Labour. From what I can gather, this is purely based on a vague idea that it's 'a bit common'.

We make it onto the aeroplane, with me now trying to hide the *Mail* amid all the hand luggage. It's bad enough to have to buy it, now I have to be seen with it, FFS. I also bought Nan a coffee, which now she doesn't want.

'It's just so big. Why do coffees these days have to be so big?'

I'm not going to argue with that one. I totally agree.

Nan genuflects as we get onto the plane. Ann and Rose are in the row behind us; I find myself sitting in the middle seat, in between Nan and an Indian lady of about Nan's age. Her name is Mrs Sharma, and I will discover later that Mrs Sharma's daughter-in-law works in my office.

Mrs Sharma's presence seems to spark off a sense of competition between the two old ladies on either side of me. Every time my nan and I start a conversation, Mrs Sharma asks me if I can help her use the headphones or take the lid off her yoghurt.

'You're a good girl. Come and see me at my flat when we arrive in Goa. Come to the gates and ask security for Mrs Sharma. They all know me.'

I nod and smile and fail to make it through more than three minutes of a film at a time without someone tapping me on the arm and asking me how long it is until we arrive and why is aeroplane coffee so bad and what is that you're watching and how long until we arrive.

After a while Nan doesn't like being upstaged and fortunately Mrs Sharma falls asleep, so Nan and I can gossip about her and then about all of our relatives who we saw at Christmas. I really do love my nan. She is an excellent person to gossip with.

Then we have another minor drama when the person in front of Nan has the audacity to put their seat back so they can go to sleep. I have rarely seen a woman so outraged.

'Nan, don't worry about it. Shall we just swap seats?'

'No. I'm not having that. It's not fair. I'm calling the stewardess and asking her to tell them to stop it. This is ridiculous.'

'Nan, I know it's annoying, but I don't think you can – '

It's too late. She's already pressed the button and is making a face I know better than to argue with. An extremely nice stewardess explains that she knows it's annoying but she can't ask them not to. Nan and I swap seats. She remains outraged.

However, by the time we are due to land – despite our very, very long day – we are in a state of high excitement. We will be landing in India! I have never set foot in India before, and this heralds a trip of great adventure and family history and maybe even – finally – self-discovery!

We pull in to land and I brace myself for the wheels hitting the ground. Instead, the plane swoops sharply back upwards and there is a collective gasp across the cabin.

'Is that supposed to happen?' Nan asks, reaching into her handbag for her Valium.

Mrs Sharma clutches at my arm convulsively.

'I'm sure it's fine,' I tell them both, inwardly resigning myself to imminent death. A relief, in so many ways.

While we circle Goa Airport repeatedly, an announcement kicks in.

'Sorry about that,' says the captain. 'We need to make another attempt at landing as there are dogs loose on the runway.'

'Dogs loose on the runway'? Dogs? Is this a joke? I presume this is an elaborate cover story for something that has gone horribly wrong. How can there be dogs loose on the runway?

'Welcome to India, darling,' my nan chuckles.

March 2017

After months and months of hanging out with The Lecturer, things had escalated. We saw each other most days; we frequently stayed up texting until 4 a.m. Sometimes we'd both press play on horror films at the same time in our respective beds, and chat throughout.

I'd grown fond of him, to the point where I now couldn't imagine my life without him. For his part, he constantly told me I was wonderful and beautiful; he found it so hard to talk to people except for me, I knew more about him than anyone else on the face of the planet.

One night while drinking cocktails and putting the world to rights, nose-to-nose on a sofa, we finally kissed. And I suddenly felt like I never wanted to kiss anyone else again. I looked at his face and I truly wondered how I never noticed he was so fucking beautiful, back at the beginning. I have always been one for the whirlwind; I never really believed someone could grow on you. But this one sneaked up on me. I appeared to be, somehow, in love with him.

I texted him when I got home that night: We need to talk about What Happened.

He replied: Lunch tomorrow? I'll buy you beer and a hotdog. See you in a few hours, lovely Ellie.

Despite my hangover, I woke up the next morning in a state of high excitement. It was unseasonably sunny, which I took to be an excellent omen, as I put on a 1950s sundress and lipstick. I texted Emma, who had long predicted that I would end up marrying The Lecturer.

'OMG, I was right! It's finally happening. Let me know how it goes – I'm going to need every detail. Fuck, he's been after you for so long, he's going to think it's Christmas!!!'

The morning at work was interminable. I was incapable of getting anything done, as I kept putting on more lipstick and counting down the minutes.

We arranged to meet in our usual spot, and we walked in the sunshine along the South Bank, where we sat outside and he bought me the promised beer and hotdog.

'So, about last night . . .' I said.

'Yes. I believe you might have some questions for me.'

'Well, more of a statement. Lecturer, it turns out that I seem to have fallen in love with you.'

I waited for him to be delighted.

'Oh, Ellie. I'm so sorry. I did not foresee this . . .'

It transpired that he was in the middle of some sort of trial separation from the long-term girlfriend I thought he'd long ago split up from. He was apparently 'confused' about life. He had thought our increasingly flirtatious friendship was a safe space because I would never be interested in 'someone like him'.

'You're wonderful and I'm regretting this even as I'm saying it,' he told me. 'But I'm afraid I'm no use to you. We both know you could do far better. Besides, be honest, how long would it be before someone like you got bored with someone like me?'

'But . . .'

'No. Don't.'

We walked back to work in silence. I texted Emma to say the grand declaration had not gone according to plan.

'Do you need wine?' she asked.

'I think I just need to go home and cry.'

I did exactly that. And then I told The Lecturer I didn't want to talk to him for a while and got straight onto Tinder, where I rushed headlong into a terrible mistake.

June 2017

Flash-forward a few months later, I was about to turn thirty-six and I needed a break. I'd pushed The Lecturer as far back in my mind as he would go, but I'd been over-extending myself and I was at a low ebb. So I decided to spend my birthday on holiday in Spain with my grandmother.

I was in the throes of a newish but intense relationship with a man who I was tying myself in knots over, while failing to see how utterly awful and problematic both he and our relationship were. It was only afterwards that I would refer to him as The Bad Boyfriend.

The night before I went away, Bad Boyfriend and I had a Friday night out, in what was supposed to be an early celebration for my birthday. I booked a table at a restaurant I'd wanted to go to for ages. I was excited as I put on a pretty dress and my best knickers. When I arrived to meet him at the pub across the road, he was already there.

He was sitting in a corner looking like a giant elegant cat. A cat who happened to be dressed like Keith Richards circa

1969: great hair, obscenely tight trousers and a bit of eyeliner. He was the very embodiment of My Type, which I guess was part of the problem. He was also the antithesis of the bookish, slightly awkward Lecturer.

He'd bought me a pint of cider. I detest cider, but I didn't tell him that. I smiled and drank it anyway, quickly. I'd seen how temperamental he could be. I wanted this to be a lovely evening; I didn't want to get off on the wrong foot. More than that, I just really, really wanted this to work.

'Happy birthday, sweetheart.' He smiled and handed me a paper bag.

I was surprised and delighted in equal measure. He could be *so* lovely. That was also part of the problem. I've never met anybody capable of being so charming.

Inside the bag was a beautiful rose quartz necklace and an obscure, out-of-print book I had happened to mention on our first date.

'I can't believe it! How did you . . . ?'

'Well, it took a bit of finding, but I called this antique bookseller in Hastings and . . . Anyway, I can't reveal my secret methods. You might go off me. Happy birthday.'

'How did you even remember?'

'Actually, I liked you so much that first night we met, I made a note on my phone so that I'd remember it. I decided there and then that I'd buy it for you on your birthday.'

It was the best first date I'd ever had. We went to a fancy cocktail bar and spent the entire evening dancing in the toilets because the music in there was better; it was the most fun I've ever had on a date.

'So, what are you doing for the next twenty-five years?' he had asked me at the end of it.

'Pfft, why so pessimistic? Make it forty.'

At the beginning, he would ring me twice a day and play me obscure Bowie B-sides and tell me I was the coolest girl he'd ever met. We skipped to the 'eating takeaway curry in bed' stage of things by about our fourth date. He would wear my pyjamas and we'd watch Netflix on my laptop. It was so cosy. It was all a great relief, to be honest. We had only been dating for a couple of months, but he kept telling me how committed he was to making our relationship work. He told me I was exactly what he had been looking for.

After a long spell of knocking about with indifferent and unsuitable men, and the eventual disappointment with The Lecturer, this had felt like the light at the end of the tunnel, the easy answer I'd been looking for.

But lately, things had felt like they were going wrong. He had been saying he wasn't sure he was over his ex. He had been ringing me up crying in the middle of the night a lot, and shouting at me for no reason. He didn't think he could handle a relationship after all. It felt like trying to hold water in my cupped hands.

I was determined to make tonight a great success.

'Anyway, how has your day been?' I asked.

'Terrible. Fucking shit. I was trying to be cheerful because it's nearly your birthday and you're going away and leaving me, but now you've asked, I just don't know if I can do it.'

'What's the matter? Can I help?'

'I doubt it. You wouldn't understand. I've had a tough day at work and my ex is being impossible and . . .'

He proceeded to talk for the next hour about the problems he'd been having with his ex. He made me read a whole string of text messages from her, which was a bit weird, but I decided it was probably better to be included in this saga rather than left out. Maybe it was a good sign.

'Um. I'm really sorry to interrupt,' I said eventually, 'but we'd better go. Our dinner reservation was ten minutes ago and I don't know how long they'll hold the table.'

'Actually, I think I'm too stressed to eat. I can't really manage food,' he said. 'Is it cool with you if we skip dinner? You don't mind, do you?'

'Oh . . . Of course, no problem. It's cool.'

As far I was concerned, it was always fucking cool. In reality, I was surprised he could hear me over the sound of my stomach rumbling. But he was very thin and I was worried he might think I was disgusting if I admitted I was really looking forward to eating dinner.

So, instead of having a lovely romantic meal in the restaurant I so carefully chose for the occasion, he carried on bitching about his ex while drinking heavily, and I tried my best to look sympathetic and not hungry.

I was relieved when he finally changed the subject, but it was in an unexpected direction that wasn't really much more positive.

'By the way, just so you know, I don't think we should sleep together tonight. I'm too stressed. I need a break. I'm not coming home with you.'

'Um, OK. Cool.'

'Let's just get really fucking drunk.'

'Um, OK. Cool.'

We drank more cider, then we drank some trendy gin in an awful bar, and eventually ended up in a pub where he started buying tequila shots. At some point late in the evening, we ran into a friend of his.

'This is Eleanor,' he said. 'She's a writer.'

He liked telling people I was a writer. It was just me actually doing writing that he didn't like. I hadn't been doing much writing lately, because every time I tried to do something that didn't revolve around him, some sort of drama would kick off in his life that required my full attention. If I said I couldn't see him because I was doing something else, sometimes he'd call me every few minutes throughout the evening. Sometimes he'd ignore me, and that would make me so anxious I couldn't concentrate on anything else anyway. It was exhausting. I was too tired to write.

This friend was someone he'd told me a lot about, someone important to him. The friend happened to be reading a book I had read; this was my chance to show that I could be fun and cool and get on with his friends! We ended up discussing books and our favourite writers. I did my best to include Bad Boyfriend in the conversation, but it became more and more difficult. He'd gone all monosyllabic and teenage.

Suddenly he downed his drink and stood up. He banged his glass down on the table, as hard and dramatically, and as close to my face, as possible.

'Fine, I get it. I'll just leave you two to it. Have a great fucking night, yeah?'

He had stormed out the door before I'd quite processed what the hell had just happened.

I abandoned my bag and my jacket, and apologised hastily to his friend as I chased after Bad Boyfriend as fast as I possibly could. I found him angrily smoking a cigarette at the end of the road. The look on his face made me burst into tears.

'You're supposed to be with *me*,' he said.

'I . . . I was just trying to make conversation with your friend.'

'You know it makes me feel left out when you talk about all that bullshit stuff you like. I don't know all those books and films you're always going on about. It's not my fault, I've always had to work too hard. I haven't had the advantages you've had. You know that. So I don't understand. Why would you behave like this?'

I tried to stop crying and I inwardly told myself, sternly, not to apologise. He should be apologising to me. I knew that. I didn't deserve any of this. If this relationship was going to work – and I still really, really wanted it to – I needed to develop some boundaries. I spent a lot of time thinking about boundaries, on the nights when he would ring me up crying at 3 a.m., and I'd be so tired I could barely get through the next day at work.

'I'm sorry,' I said. It just slipped out.

'Hey, sweetheart. It's OK, don't cry. I forgive you. Shall we go back to your place?'

I was so relieved to be back in favour, I didn't even mind that this point of the evening was often when the real problems started.

He always had sex with me like he hated me. The first time, it started off OK and then got a bit rough and he apologised afterwards, said we were both too drunk and had got carried away. The second time it was normal and fine, and I breathed a sigh of relief. It stayed normal for a while, until once he whispered in my ear that I was a dirty whore. I so clearly remember the sudden disappointment I felt. Things had been going so well. So I ignored it and hoped maybe I'd heard him wrong. He often claimed I had heard things wrong.

The next time he whispered in my ear that I was a dirty whore who wanted to be raped. By then, I'd done such a good job of ignoring all red flags, I guessed I might as well just carry on and keep pretending not to hear him. After that it steadily got worse but – in a very twisted and self-abasing sort of logic – I guessed I'd kind of consented to it by ignoring it in the beginning.

He would hold me down and spit in my face and call me a dirty animal. He had a particular fondness for inserting inanimate objects into unexpected orifices with no prior warning. Sometimes this was done in a fashion that would leave me crying on the toilet for a good couple of days afterwards. Once he shoved his fingers so hard down my throat I couldn't swallow properly the next day. At least this time, he didn't stick a cucumber up my arse. I had managed to distract him recently by purchasing quite a small rose quartz dildo. Life had been a lot more comfortable since I did that. We were both into crystals.

He always said it was my fault for 'having this effect' on him. He didn't even want to come back here, remember?

I tried to bring all this up once, suggesting we instigate some rules or at least maybe a safe word. Like 'macaroni' or 'umbrella' or something, as 'fuck, you're really hurting me' didn't appear to be working. In fact, it seemed to make things worse. He reluctantly said something long-winded and incomprehensible about how I should understand his sexual preferences were separate from what he was really like as a person. I didn't really know what to do with that, so I probably just muttered 'cool' and asked him if he wanted another glass of wine.

I'd always prided myself on being open-minded and he was an expert in making me feel like I was being the unreasonable one. I tried to tell myself I was being 'adventurous'. Nervousness can feel a bit like excitement, and I started to get the two mixed up.

It was always worse if we were both drunk, which we frequently were. Sometimes when we woke up in the morning and he was nice to me, and he brought me a cup of tea in bed, I would wonder if I'd been imagining things. He's willowy and softly spoken; if you met him, you'd think he was a gentle hippie. Then later, after he had left, I'd realize I was bleeding and covered in bruises, and it was all real.

One morning we woke up and the bed was soaked in blood; we were both covered in it. He was so solicitous about my gynaecological health, he actually managed to convince me it had been nothing to do with what he'd been doing to me the night before.

'I think you should go to the doctor, darling. It's like a fucking Tarantino movie in here. Has this ever happened to you before? It's not normal, you should get it checked out. I'll come with you if you want.'

I was nearly thirty-six years old. I had never had a properly Bad Boyfriend before. I had always thought most people were nice, or at least ineptly doing their best, like me. I guess that's why it took me so long to realize how bad this was. I'd never heard words like 'gaslighting' and 'narcissist'. Up until then, I'd been lucky. I had no frame of reference for such things.

I genuinely didn't want to lose him, this beautiful charming man who appeared to be a lot madder than I had realized and was possibly trying to systematically break me down, bit by bit.

I was invested by now. I had believed him when he said we were perfect for each other. At first, I had felt seen and understood, for the first time in such a long time. I was so grateful to him.

He was the first man I had really opened up to in a long time. I told him all about my stepdad: how mad I went and how much I still missed him. I really thought I could trust him. He was a person who'd been through a lot and had a turbulent family history. His 'Dickensian orphan life', as he called it. I told him everything. I cried and he stroked my hair and told me I didn't deserve any of this.

He was convinced I should try to get back in touch with

Stepdad, pointing out I'd always regret it if something happened and I missed the chance. Both of his parents were dead, so he should know.

'I'll help you,' he said. 'I'm here for you.'

I wasn't sure how things slipped this far downhill. It had happened so gradually, I didn't notice it. I guess that's how it always happens.

'Have a lovely holiday,' he said when he left my house the next morning. 'Lucky you, I've never had a holiday. I've always had to work too hard. I think it will be good for us to have a break from each other.'

After he left, as usual, I felt unsettled and found myself crying for no reason, and not just because of the inevitable post-sex bleeding-when-I-shit situation. What did 'having a break' mean? Was I allowed to text him? I didn't like to ask in case it made him cross. This was terrible timing to be parted from him for two weeks. Things felt so shaky. I was very anxious.

I was still hopeful that I could make things work, so I couldn't tell any of my friends about this. Besides, it was all so nebulous. Sometimes we had rough sex that went a bit too far. He hadn't *actually* ever hit me; he threatened to once, during a minor argument that escalated quickly, but afterwards he insisted that I had misheard him.

I didn't know how to put any of this into words. But I knew exactly what my friends would say. Worse, I knew exactly what I would say to them if the roles were reversed. I skirted around a few things, mentioned he could be a bit moody, said the sex was a bit weird but 'I was mostly into it'. I couldn't tell them what was really going on. You know, that might make things awkward at our future wedding!

And so I put Bad Boyfriend to the back of my mind as much as I could, as I packed my suitcase and prepared to spend my birthday on holiday with my grandmother. We were going to her house in Spain, a holiday villa in a vast complex of holiday villas, many of which are inhabited by the over-eighties. I love it. Seriously, love it. You can walk to a bar and a shop at the end of the road in approximately twenty seconds. That's kind of it.

It would be just me and my nan for a week, and then Auntie Rose was coming out for the second week.

Turned out, this was the ideal holiday to have at such a weird time in my life. For a start, my nan has a plentiful supply of Valium that she doesn't mind sharing. We had a couple of pills each with a gin and tonic on the flight and from then onwards drank gin with our lunch every day. It was the first time I'd had a fortnight off work maybe ever, and it turned out going away with old people was really relaxing. It forces you to slow down, which I am usually terrible at.

However, I missed Bad Boyfriend terribly, and spent the whole time wearing the birthday necklace he gave me and trying to think up plausible ways to text him that wouldn't make him cross that I was disturbing him when he clearly wanted a break from me (I saw a cat that looked like you

today? I was listening to that Radiohead song you like?).
Nan and I listened to Radiohead a lot on that holiday.

'It's quite good,' said Nan. 'Atmospheric. Some of it's quite
sexy.'

We spent our days lying in the sun together and reading
Jilly Cooper novels, tottering no further than the end of the
road to the bar for our lunch and dinner. I woke up early
every morning and went running in concentric circles through
the complex, past houses that looked so identical I often got
lost. When I came back, Nan would just be waking up and
I would bring her coffee and biscuits in bed before making
breakfast. We would sit about on the sunny patio drinking
coffee and eating toast and chatting for hours each day, by
which point it was nearly time for a gin.

When Auntie Rose arrived, the three of us fell into a great
routine that involved pretty much doing nothing, from our
morning coffee and digestives, through to our last post-
dinner glass of wine. Nan and Rose often stayed up later
than me, watching *Poldark* on BBC Worldwide while I went
to bed at 10 p.m. Living so slowly was soporific. At home
I have terrible trouble sleeping and never sleep through the
night. Here, I could barely keep my eyes open in the evenings.
I brought a stack of books with me and didn't finish one
of them.

I didn't need books when there was so much chatting to
be done. Turned out, the great joy of that holiday was talking
my nan and Auntie Rose and hearing their stories. With a
whole fortnight to go deep and ask the nosiest questions
imaginable after a few glasses of wine, I realized for the first

time that there was so much about our family and their lives I never knew.

Nan and I had always been close, but I'd never really delved into the past with her. This was the most time by a long way I'd ever spent with Auntie Rose. Usually I would see my aunties at Christmas and Easter, weddings and funerals, where there are always a million other people around. My family is huge and complicated, mostly due to the fact that nearly everyone has been married more than once.

Auntie Rose is great company and a huge amount of fun. She's always up for anything; she rented a car in Spain and drove us around on trips to the beach and the market. My nan's cool older sister, she has both an air of properness and a very naughty sense of humour. She was considered a great beauty when they were young, and she still acts like it, with an impressive combination of flirting and imperiousness. She's given up now, but she smoked like a chimney for most of her life, so has a wonderful gravelly speaking voice that makes everything sound like a sexy secret.

Like my nan, she's spent all of her life working as well as being a mother and grandmother. She's a great golfer; she loves a gin and tonic. Now that she's older, she's still involved with the WI and goes to tai chi once a week. Since her husband died, she moved to Dorset, where she lives with her son, his wife and his family. She drives her teenage grandkids to school every day.

Rose is always up for just one more drink. She is a woman who knows her worth and does not take any shit. She's a stickler for manners and has a stern side, but she's also given to winking and bursting out laughing – especially around my nan. When they're together, the years fall away and the two of them revert to giggling, bickering schoolgirls. When they were at school, Rose always used to look out for my nan and was often the one to speak up for her, as my nan was a much shyer child. Rose has never been shy.

When she realized I was genuinely interested in her stories, they kept on coming. I hung off every word.

'Did I ever tell you about when I was living in the YWCA in Mumbai?' she would ask me out of nowhere. 'It was quite an adventure. Most girls didn't live on their own in those days, but I went out and got myself a job as a secretary and organized my own accommodation. I just wanted to be where the excitement was. I thought working as a secretary was a good bet, as it would mean I could be around interesting people. Back in England I ended up working in the City and sharing a flat in Kensington with a model. But that's another story for another day, darling.'

I couldn't get enough of these stories. It is unbelievable to me that all of this happened within living memory, how different and exotic their lives were, and at the same time how much common ground we have.

It was the perfect way of putting things into perspective. It fully struck me for the first time that they had been through more than I had ever imagined. These women were *staunch*.

So, I spent my thirty-sixth birthday on the beach, drinking margaritas and eating paella for lunch, asking Nan and Rose a million questions about their lives. Once I started, I grew even more insatiably curious about what life was like when they were kids, what it was like moving to this country for the first time as teenagers, how they met their husbands, how they felt about the world. I wanted to know everything.

Lest this all sound too worthy, I also forced my nan to take approximately one million photographs of me posing with a cocktail in my bikini, until we got a good one. I posted it on Instagram in a sad bid for attention and to convince myself I was still (relatively) young and hot, even though I was now officially nearer to forty than thirty, and I was spending my birthday with two octogenarians. Even though I had a boyfriend who seemed to hate me a bit.

To be fair, Bad Boyfriend did text me on my birthday. He said he hoped I was having a lovely day, then went on to tell me at length that he was most emphatically *not*. He'd had another bust-up with his ex, as well as some complicated drama at work, and something about having to build some shelves, which seemed to have been extremely stressful for him.

He sent me a picture of himself wearing my dressing gown, which I had lent him the morning I went away.

'Isn't that sweet?' I said to Nan, showing her the picture.

She was furious. My nan is very rarely furious. I was taken aback. The last time this happened was when she threw the Christmas tree at me and my cousin Nic in 1995. We were being right little bitches, to be fair. We were both so horrified that we had made Nan lose her temper, we still talk about it in hushed tones.

'I bought you that dressing gown last Christmas!' she cried.

'It was from The White Company, it cost nearly £80! You don't just give your things away to any Tom, Dick or Harry you've only known for a few months!'

'But . . . It's this whole thing, you see. He always wears it when he comes over and because I was going away, we – '

'No, Ells. I'm sorry to say it, but someone has to. He's not for you and that's all there is to it.'

I'd love to say this inspired me to go home and break up with Bad Boyfriend. Actually, I got home from Spain and never heard from him again. I should be grateful for the lucky escape – now I most definitely am, now that he seems like nothing more than a very distant bad dream – but at the time I was distraught over it.

I never did get that dressing gown back. He's still got my *Grey Gardens* DVD too. This probably makes me the very opposite of staunch. It also serves to demonstrate that my nan is always right.

Present Day

So, when Nan and Rose decided they wanted to go back to India, possibly – let's face it – one last time, I was the obvious choice to come with them to help.

We all got on so well in Spain, and I was really good at running around after them and bringing them cups of tea in the morning. My Auntie Ann decided to come with us on our journey of Indian discovery too. As she is their younger half-sister, she is a youngster for me to hang out with – she's only seventy-two. While I was growing up, Ann lived in Hong Kong. So she was my glamorous, distant great-aunt who we only saw on very special occasions. I had never spent very much time with her before.

All of them were born in India: Nan and Rose were teenagers when they left, and Ann was only two and has no memory of living there. Nan has been back to India a lot over the years and has kept up speaking Urdu (mostly with her local Asian friends), but the last time she went was ten years ago. As she's got further into her eighties, she's been putting off the hassle of a long-haul flight. However, recently she has decided it's now or never. 'Never' is a word that has rarely entered her vocabulary, so by default, it's now.

Much of this was led by Rose, who hasn't been back to India since the day she left, aged eighteen. She's never been one to dwell on the past. Besides, she had a husband who would never have considered a trip to India (or wanted her to go alone). Now he has passed away and Rose has a bit of money, this is what she wants to do with it. Finally – seventy years after leaving – she has a hankering to make one last trip. It's some kind of primal urge that seems to have set in late in life: the idea that if they don't go now, they may never again set foot in the country where they were born.

Like me, Ann has been brought in by Nan and Rose as part of their plan. Ann is not only much younger than her siblings, but having been very athletic all her life, is in great physical shape. She is a former runner and hockey-player, now avid walker and golfer. Not only is she the youngest by a long way, but she looks even more so – she has maintained a very sporty figure and has lovely glossy dark hair, the combination of which lead people generally to assume she is somewhere around the fifty mark, when in fact, her eldest daughter is fifty.

Ann was the cleverest daughter, and she holds herself with the confidence that this standing deserves. As well as being stunning, she is one of the sharpest women I have ever met. She is witty and always interesting, challenging company, with an incredible breadth of knowledge, due to her genuinely diverse interests. She loves Virginia Woolf, goes to every film and art exhibition in London, travels the world and has an encyclopaedic knowledge of most sports. In short, Ann is the one you want on your pub quiz team.

Although I'm there to do the heavy lifting, I suspect Nan and Rose (quite fairly) figured that, as I have absolutely no common sense, we would also need Ann onside. I have to admit, it was an inspired decision. She is a retired teacher: very practical and no-nonsense, and keeps all of us in check. Also like me, Ann is a willing participant in this plan – she is well travelled and has lived in several countries, but she has never returned to India.

Their parents never went back after they left, because logistically and financially, it would not have been an option. Since then, time has gone by and nobody ever quite got around to it, but with the passing years, family history has somehow become more important. I guess that's the way it works – the older we get, the more we want to be connected to the past, even if we never really cared before.

So now here we are – to varying degrees, the blind leading the blind. Or at least the blind leading the elderly, high-maintenance and not very mobile.

As we sit on a bus at Goa Airport for two hours, while nobody seems to have any idea what's actually going on, it occurs to me that being a Victorian lady's companion was probably quite a lot easier in Spain, where we were in my nan's house and didn't have to walk more than ten metres at a time, and even then it was only for a gin and a *hamburguesa* at the end of the road. Oh, and as you will have gleaned from my unnecessary use of the word *hamburguesa* (the word amuses me), I got an 'A' in GCSE Spanish. True story. My Urdu isn't so hot. My plan is to rely on my nan but, although she speaks fluent Urdu, the main local dialect in Goa is Konkani, so we might all struggle.

I've never been to India before; I don't know how it works. This becomes immediately apparent. The bus we are on is approximately two hundred years old and is somehow boiling hot, airless and too cold all at once. Sweat is pouring down my back but I am shivering. There are dogs running around outside everywhere, turns out that wasn't a made-up story by the pilot. People are shouting at each other and I can't understand a word. I'm not even sure we're on the right bus; we were hustled onto it by a man who forcibly took our suitcases then demanded money for him and 'his friend'. It's nearly 2 a.m.

The bus eventually starts up like something out of *Wacky Races*. Even at this time, the roads are hectic – with the odd car, but mostly with mopeds, cows and dogs. We go from the airport highways and billboards into smaller, twisty roads where the houses – a dizzying mixture of grand houses and shacks in a jumble – are all covered in fairy lights. It's hard to tell whether people are very into kitsch home design, or if they all still have their Christmas decorations up. Being of Portuguese influence, Goa is a very Christian area of India. There are Christmas decorations, fairy lights, neon signs, and the particularly garish Café Ganesh, which is a shack with all of the above plus a giant rotating 3D Coca-Cola logo on the roof.

As we swerve around the pot-holed, fairy-lit roads, my nan immediately starts to feel carsick, which she assures me never usually happens.

'Have you got a plastic bag?' she whispers to me.

We get one off the panicky driver just in time for Nan to vomit into it while Rose loudly asks what's going on. Instructed by Ann, he takes a detour and drops us off first.

When we booked the trip, we realized that we had quite a lot of practical requirements. If you're going to India when you're in your late eighties, the checklist turns into something akin to Mariah Carey's rider. We needed to be on the ground floor, as Rose was not so hot on stairs these days. We needed two adjoining twin rooms. We needed to be near the beach and town, as walking long distances was out.

This was how we ended up choosing Goa, and we found a hotel that not only managed to meet all of these requirements, but provided golf carts to transport you between the pool, the beach and the restaurant. It was much grander than we intended but we (well, my nan) decided to go for it.

So when we arrive at the hotel, with a troupe of security guards letting us in through the grand front gates, I guess it must be fancy but we're all too tired to take it in.

Nan's still being sick into a leaky carrier bag as our suitcases are whisked away and somebody hands us coconuts with straws in and puts shell necklaces over our heads. Later, I ask her what happened to the sick-bag and she says someone discreetly took it out of her hands and she was too embarrassed to say anything. I absolutely don't blame her. I'd have done exactly the same. I was quite glad I wasn't holding it, to be honest.

The hotel lobby is vast, with shiny marble floors, fragrant with incense and, even at 3 a.m., crowded full of smiling staff. We are quite shell-shocked.

As we are taken to our adjoining rooms – one for me and Nan to share, one for Rose and Ann – it becomes apparent that there is a problem. I just want to get into bed. And, let's face it, I'm the youngest here by over forty years and I'm not the one who's recently had a bag of sick taken off them. We all really just want to go to bed.

Except it seems, surprisingly, my nan. She seems to get a new lease of life as soon as she clocks the adjoining rooms, each with one king-size bed, rather than the requested twin beds.

'We can figure it out in the morning,' I say hopefully.

'Absolutely not.'

Staff are duly called in and it transpires there has been a mix-up and there are no suitable rooms available. There is a tired, passive-aggressive row about this, while I try to diffuse the tension by smiling too much and declaring 'it's fine, really!' and the others glare at me. They're right; I'm not helping at all.

'We can just share!' I suggest.

'We cannot,' says Nan.

Rather than agree to share the vast king-size bed with me, Nan asks if an alternative sleeping arrangement can be found. The staff tell her they can sort it out immediately.

And this is how I end up spending the forthcoming weeks in what is widely regarded as the second-best hotel in all of India (Nan tells me with good authority that the Oberoi is slightly nicer), sleeping on a child-sized camp bed.

What the fuck have I done?

December 1947

Imagine Glasgow, in January. Pretty fucking cold, right? Now imagine it if you had only ever lived in India for your entire life and you didn't even own a winter coat. Or a pair of tights.

My family originally emigrated from the UK to Rawalpindi in India, in the nineteenth century, when my great-great-great-grandparents moved there to build railways.

My great-grandmother, Dolly, was born in 1905, technically a third-generation immigrant. She did not set foot in the UK until she was forty-two years old, where she had to start an entirely new life. As I remember her, she was a tiny but very spirited old lady in a flowered housecoat. She was definitely staunch.

Dolly lived until she was ninety-seven, vocally hated my Doc Martens when I was a teenager and always beat me at *Countdown*. She had a creepy picture of Jesus, bleeding far too realistically in his crown of thorns, on her bedroom wall that we were all frightened of. We all lived in fear of her asking us to 'just nip upstairs and fetch my handbag for me' because nobody wanted to deal with Jesus. He almost definitely had eyes that would follow you around the room.

Dolly was married for the first time to William James, who was by all accounts not a very nice man. She had her six eldest children with him: Clara (the staunchest woman I have ever met), Rose, Dorothea (my nan), and Bill, plus two others who died in early infancy.

Rose told me her abiding memory of her biological father was that she wasn't allowed to sit on his lap as a child in case she somehow spoiled his perfectly pressed trousers. He was a dandy, a philanderer and, reading between the lines, a bit of a dick.

In 1944, in a bold move for the time, Dolly left him for Chum (whose real name was Samuel, but everyone called him Chum – I guess because, as I remember, he was basically the nicest man in the world). He was also younger than her and very handsome. I remember him as a dapper gent with slicked-back hair, who could play the harmonica, had a lovely singing voice and adored children. Whenever he won at cards, he would split his winnings between the kids.

William James, on the other hand, shook his teenage daughters by the hand and never saw them again.

Anyway, Dolly took the children with her and she and Chum had two more: Ann and Sam. They remained evidently and very sweetly in love until death did them part – Chum when I was sixteen, Dolly when I was twenty-one.

They met in Rawalpindi, then lived for a time in Lahore

– both of which were in the north but are now in Pakistan – and settled in Pune, which is further away in the south, near Mumbai. The family lived a pretty charmed life in British India. It was a life built on very problematic colonialism, but I can't deny it sounded like a good time.

'We treated our servants very well. They adored us,' was the sort of thing I would hear Dolly say. 'They all cried when we left.'

They didn't realize they were subscribing to an oppressive regime; it was the life they were born into. Like a lot of other British people in India at that time, they were living a better life than they would have been back home. They didn't think to question any of it.

Yes, it was a life of servants and hanging at The Burt Institute (white people only), going to dances and putting on plays. Basically, they pretended they were in Britain; so much so that everyday life sounds like it was some sort of Merchant Ivory film. It was all afternoon tea and croquet on the lawn, and Cook asking what the menu and seating plan should be for supper this evening, madam.

The small children were brought up by *ayahs*, whom they adored. At six, they were sent away to an English-style boarding school in the mountains, where they would spend nine months of the year.

For the other three, they were spoiled rotten at home. The servants would bring them *chota hasri* ('small breakfast'), which was served in bed and followed by *burra hasri* (yep, 'big breakfast'). They would be brought tiffin tins of curry and rice by a bearer for lunch, followed by a grand afternoon tea on the lawn, and a full 'English' dinner. No wonder my grandmother says she was quite a podgy child.

The family's household staff consisted of the aforementioned *ayahs*, a cook, a sweeper, a gardener, a bearer (whose jobs included laying the table and washing up) and a *bishti* (or 'water bearer', whose job was to carry water in a goat skin on his back).

Nan's best friend was the cook's daughter, even though this was slightly disapproved of on all sides. Nan was the naughty one. She spent most of her time hanging in the servants' quarters, speaking Urdu with them and generally making a nuisance of herself. While I don't think this was her taking some sort of political stance on the upstairs/downstairs divide, rather just the result of her chatty nature, it does mean that she's hung onto more of the language and culture and still considers herself more 'Indian' than her siblings.

Partition happened in August 1947, the end of British India and the division of the land into India and Pakistan. It was messy and awful and shameful. Over a million people died and millions more were displaced.

By December 1947, the family would have to flee their home in India. Despite considering themselves very much 'British', they had never set foot in Britain. And so they prepared to go 'back' to a country they had never been to, as refugees with nowhere to live. And, inconveniently, none of them had ever even owned a coat . . .

December 2016

My nan is my mum's mum, and it's funny that I should end up finding out so much about that side of the family, as it is actually my dad who got me interested in our family history.

There have been very few discernible upsides to the events of the past few years, but my relationship with my dad is possibly the biggest one. We've always got on, but we have never been as close as we are now.

I used to think my dad and I were totally different, probably because I take so much after my mother. My mum and I look alike, we have identical handwriting, our voices sound so similar that people can't tell us apart on the phone. If my mum is going through something, I feel as if I am going through it myself, and vice versa. Somewhere along the line, I'm pretty sure there was a psychic cord somewhere that never quite got cut the way it was supposed to.

On the other hand, you wouldn't pick my dad out of a line-up. My sister has his blue eyes, freckles and teeth, but I got nothing. As a teenager, rather insultingly to both of my parents, I used to ask my mum if she was *sure* my dad was my real father. Was there any possibility that she had somehow got this wrong? This was mainly inspired by – having watched *Empire Records* – wanting to be just like Liv Tyler, who had famously only discovered as a teenager that Steven Tyler from Aerosmith was her biological father. This situation sounded rather glamorous to me.

My parents split up when I was eleven and both married other people extremely quickly afterwards. My sister and I would go to stay with my dad, who now lived in our house with my stepmother and two young stepbrothers, every other weekend. I was moved into a converted bedroom in the cellar and we'd all make Cinderella jokes.

I was the eldest, the independent one who just got on with it. My dad and I got on, but I was never really an adoring daddy's girl like my younger sister was. During my teenage years, we spent much of our time low-level arguing that I (understandably, at that age) wanted to spend all my weekend time with my friends, while he (also understandably) thought that I should be making the most of the limited family time we had together. I've never spoken to my dad much about it, but it probably wasn't very nice for him that I was living with my mum's new husband the rest of the time, eating dinner with him five nights a week and having him help me with my homework.

My dad moved to rural North Wales when I was at university and we would mostly stay in touch on the phone. He had my stepmum, Sue, and before too long I had K, and neither of us had to worry about each other too much.

Sue died suddenly and far too young, when I was thirty. I went to stay with my dad for a little while afterwards, after the funeral, and stayed on after K and my sister had both left. I knew it was time to leave when he started asking me to do his ironing, but I was glad I could be there during that time. My brilliant stepbrother Simon then moved back home with him for a while and heroically taught himself to iron shirts properly from a YouTube video, as well as many, many other things.

From then on, my dad and I started speaking more frequently. I liked to make sure that he was OK as he was more in need of the company than before. We found we got on so well, we chatted far more than we were required to for these ostensible purposes.

K and I had just moved into our new house when my dad came to stay the night, saying that he had a date the following evening. We drank wine and discussed the new *Guardian* dating profile he had just set up.

By the time K and I finally broke up, Dad was engaged to Fiona, his *Guardian Soulmates* girlfriend. Fiona has been one of the other main upsides to the past few years, a wonderful addition to the team of staunch women in my family. Fortunately for me, she is a truly lovely person, and is the sort of generous-spirited stepmother who doesn't find it too odd that my dad speaks on the phone to his elder daughter nearly every day, often for two hours at a time.

I now actively look forward to my conversations with my dad, and miss him terribly if he goes away on holiday and I don't speak to him for a week. We talk a lot about politics, quite a bit about writing, generally about big ideas rather than minutiae. Surprisingly, even to me, we talk at length and in some detail about my love life.

I know there are some people who think this is over-sharing, considering he is my father and all. The thing is, my dad is nosy and can't resist asking me questions, and I am apparently incapable of answering a direct question with anything other than the truth.

The great thing for me is I have learned a lot about my father during the process. He often punctuates my tales of dating woe with anecdotes from his own life. Thus, for the first time, I am now aware of his regrets about his marriage to my mum, how he didn't consider himself a fully functional adult until he was in his forties despite the fact that I was born when he was thirty-two, that he is now critical of his own hands-off Eighties parenting style with my sister and me, and how he felt about embarking on dating again when he was in his sixties. It's been illuminating for us both. Occasionally I feel sad this didn't happen sooner, but I guess a lot of people don't come to appreciate their parents fully until they are proper grown-ups themselves.

My dad is academic by nature and loves a research project. In recent years, he has been doing the classic retirement project of investigating our family history. He assured me this is something that most people become more interested in the older they get, and the more they are confronting their own mortality.

At first, I was slightly sneery about this and opined that people are only ever keen to explore their family trees because they're hoping they will uncover something extraordinary that will prove that they are interesting by association. For most people, surely, this was more than likely to be a disappointment. However, as time went on, I had to admit that I was wrong and my dad was right. Of course. He not only uncovered some fascinating stories about his side of the family, he totally sparked my interest in the subject. It became yet another topic that we would discuss frequently and at great length.

For Christmas, my dad made me, my sister and stepbrothers two family albums each. These are the best presents I have ever received, and the work he put into them is phenomenal. Each of us had an album dedicated to our family history, and an individual album each about ourselves.

The family album went back to 1600 and included stories I had never heard before, my favourite relative being Dennis, a pianist who played on Clacton Pier, despite having lost a finger in World War One. Apparently he had a 'racy' wife.

As we got closer to my own generation, and the people I actually knew, I was surprised by how emotional I found it all. This was really what inspired me to find out more about the family members around me while I was still lucky enough to have them around. I wish I could talk to my dad's parents about some of the stories he unearthed. I can't bear the idea of these stories – the hopes and dreams, the great loves and break-ups – being lost.

'You should talk more to your nan and Rose about their side of the family – there are certainly some stories there,' my dad said in passing, not realizing this would turn into a quest that would take me halfway around the world with them.

I took this idea and ran with it, embracing the idea of family stories with a zeal that some of my family began to find a bit wearing.

A few months ago, when I was staying at my sister's house, she got out our parents' old Seventies wedding album, which I had never seen before. I took one look at the first picture of them and burst into uncontrollable tears that didn't subside for about an hour.

'Oh my God, Ellie,' my sister laughed. 'I just thought we were going to have a laugh about Mum's perm and Dad's moustache.'

'It's just,' I managed to gulp, 'they really loved each other once, didn't they? Look at them. Everyone gets married with such high hopes. They had no idea what was going to happen. They thought they'd be together for ever.'

'What is *wrong* with you?'

It is testament to the work that my dad put into the albums that my famously self-contained sister did, in fact, burst into tears the first time she saw hers.

My dad had saved things that I had no idea existed. There were not only old family photographs, but also short stories I had written as a child, and my old school reports. I was extremely pleased to note that my creative writing talent had been spotted early, although my grasp of basic maths was 'shaky' and I was apparently 'suspicious of new work'.

They say that all women in the end turn into their mothers. The thing is, I have basically always *been* my mother. As I've got older, I think I've become more like my dad. Sometimes I laugh and my mum says, 'my God, it's spooky how much you sound like your father.' I recently saw a picture of myself – in the pub, clutching a full pint, and grinning broadly and crookedly – in which I am convinced I look a bit like my dad. No more unfounded Steven Tyler conspiracy theories. Seeing this slight resemblance brought me a flash of deep joy.

Whether I actually look like my dad or not is beside the point. He has, among other things, given me a mixed bag of blessings that include but are not limited to the following:

- An appreciation of Neil Young
- An endless appetite for red wine and crisps
- Deeply held and idealistic opinions
- The habit of starting a to-do list with something I've already done, for the sake of positivity
- An interest in family history that I was convinced I'd never have.

Present Day

I wake up on my camp bed on my first morning in India and I realize that our room is beautiful. It's incredible; probably the nicest place I have stayed in my entire life. It embodies ultimate hotel luxury: tasteful lighting, sleek wet room and stacks of thick white towels, and a bowl of fruit that never gets touched.

Back home, my house is grimy and damp and I can never afford to do any of the things to it that need doing; my commute means that all winter I only see my house in daylight at weekends, and by then I just want to get drunk or eat pizza in bed while watching Netflix.

This clean, bright hotel luxury is what my poor privileged basic bitch soul never realized it needed. I feel better already.

Best of all is the view from the balcony. The hotel grounds stretch out for some distance: immaculate swimming pool, palm trees and hammocks, little lanterns everywhere that are lit up at night. But beyond that, there is the beach. The sea!

I am in India.

It's early and nobody else will be up for hours, so I decide to go for a run. I am usually first up, wherever I am. Early morning is my favourite time, as long as I have no alarm and nothing I have to do. Did you know Leonard Cohen used to get up at 4 a.m. to write? He was a devotee to that half-world time between being awake and asleep. That's why I should do morning pages but I invariably wake up too late and end up having to run to the station before managing to have a cup of coffee or apply lipstick.

On the worst holiday of my life, for my sister's birthday, when nobody could know that K and I had already broken up, I would wake up determinedly earlier and earlier every morning, to avoid us having to look at each other with our eyes open, let alone touch. Every morning I would go out running for miles as it was getting light, crying behind my sunglasses, dreading going back and with no idea how we could possibly have got to this point.

Here, I am free. However, the hotel is a perfect bubble, and it strikes me that this must be much like how my grand-mother's life was during the British Raj. It's all staff saying 'good morning, madam' and nodding politely as they water the impossibly lush plants. It's not real life.

On one side of us is the beach and, on the other, the road into town; if you get close enough, you can even hear people chatting, mopeds whining and wild dogs barking. But it is all separated from us by a fence that runs the perimeter of the hotel grounds. There are guards posted at gates on each side; you have to give your room number to enter or exit the place, and cars are checked inside and out with an alarming level of detail.

I'm too jetlagged and too nervous even to venture a little way outside yet. I run slow laps around the hotel grounds, sticking to the edges like I've got some kind of Stockholm syndrome. Around the pool, the tennis courts, the spa, the restaurants. It's already hot.

I finish my run unsatisfied, with a sense of curiosity about what's on the other side of the fence.

Present Day

I head back to the room to be greeted with the daily routine that will become very familiar to me over the next few weeks. My nan and Rose faffing over what to wear to breakfast.

Anything they tell you about vanity going out the window after a certain age and how liberating it's going to be? That is utter, utter bullshit. And actually, I'm glad it is. I think there's something heartening about being in one's late eighties and still really caring about looking nice.

Nan and Rose have both brought more clothes with them than they could possibly wear. There are different shoes to go with each outfit, a variety of day and evening bags, always a pashmina 'just in case'. Little cardigans that go with particular dresses. Lipsticks in shades of coral and pink that are indistinguishable to me, but apparently very different. Necklaces with coloured glass beads that go with particular trousers, plus the inevitable matching earrings.

Then there are the patterned sundresses that they have both stockpiled in various colours from the market in Spain, which they inexplicably call 'floaters'. There is much discussion about floaters, as they each have an identical collection and want to avoid matching.

'Rosie, are you going for a floater today?' reverberates regularly through the adjoining rooms.

'Dot, I'm going for the yellow floater today. So don't wear yours!'

Incidentally, the housekeeping staff clearly think that my camp bed is for a small child and that there are in fact three people staying in the room. I am fine with this as we start getting extra bottled water and a third more of the luridly coloured marzipan sweets every day that we never touch, plus three pairs of slippers, which can only be useful.

The housekeeping staff are extremely zealous. Every day my flip-flops and trainers (the only shoes I brought with me, unlike Nan and Rose) are lined up on a mat. Pretty bookmarks are inserted into each of my stack of holiday paperbacks. Nan can't find her phone charger for three days because it has been so efficiently tidied away.

I can't help but feel they must be baffled by the sheer volume of stuff that Nan has brought with her. It's like she's moved in permanently. She was up until gone 4 a.m. on our first night, just hanging up her clothes. There's a sarong that matches every different swimsuit, and a corresponding pair of sandals and various items of jewellery.

All of this means that we won't make it to breakfast before 10 a.m., ever.

'What do you think I should wear today?'

At first, I reply in the same way I would reply to this question from any friend.

'Pfft. Who cares? Anything!'

There will then be a long explanation about exactly how wrong I am. How she can't wear the turquoise floater because she wore something too similar yesterday (what would people think?). She'll try on the pink top with her white Capri pants, but decide the proportions don't work at all, and the purple top is probably better. This necessitates a change of bra, as it absolutely must match in case a millimetre should peek out.

My first instinct is eye-rolling boredom and mild piss-taking. I wear the same trousers every day for the first week in India, alternate the few T-shirts I have brought and have the same bikini on underneath at all times. I only brought one and just wear it when I get in the shower every evening to give it a rinse, then hang it out on the balcony overnight. Boom. Job done.

I soon realize how wrong this attitude is. Lack of vanity is fine for me but it's not a virtue. As Nan tells me repeatedly – and Ann, who has a level of vanity similar to mine – 'of course you can just throw on anything when you're young; you have to make more of an effort when you get to our age'. She's right, and I also really like how she doesn't differentiate between thirty-six and seventy-two, both qualifying as 'young'.

So, anyone who tells you that you lose your vanity with age is lying, and I'm glad. It seems to me that the inverse is true. A certain type of vanity increases the older you get, which makes perfect sense.

So much of ageing involves a dispiriting feeling of invisibility. I'm feeling it already, although I have actually always prided myself on being something of a niche market. When I was younger, I always had to have something to mark me out as not caring, to show that I was out of the race and not trying to be 'pretty', so please don't bother judging me by those standards: if I wore a nice dress, I'd stick an ugly brown Oxfam granddad cardigan over the top; if I'd made an effort with my eye make-up, I'd make sure I didn't brush my hair. I have always had an absolute horror of looking 'overdone', of trying too hard. I grew up in the Nineties, when 'try-hard' was the worst insult you could say to a person, and I've never grown out of it. These days, it feels like the pressure is on all sides – we must be 'body positive' and practice radical self-love while looking effortlessly sexy at the same time.

As I've got older, I've accepted that I'm not everyone's cup of tea. I certainly don't expect well-groomed men in expensive suits to go for the woman with tattoos, who cuts her own hair and doesn't shave her armpits.

But with age I've started noticing that the pool of men is getting smaller. I sometimes see boys with skinny trousers and guitars strapped to their backs, and wonder why they aren't noticing I'm doing my sexy face at them. Then I'll remember that I'm probably fifteen years older than them and the whole thing would be grossly inappropriate. And don't get me started on the seemingly huge numbers of men *exactly my age* who have set their online dating age range as, say, twenty-five–thirty-two. I tell myself I wouldn't want to go out with those guys anyway, but it's still insulting.

My mum, who is conventionally and unarguably attractive, says the worst thing about ageing is the steadily diminishing numbers of heads that turn when you walk into a room. I can understand that. It's depressing.

This is why I love the fact that Nan and Rose are convinced that people are looking at them closely enough to care whether they wear the same dress twice in a row for breakfast. And it's true: these things come full circle. Nobody wants to be invisible, and being a middle-aged woman feeling like nobody notices you is shit. However, I soon realize that everybody *is* actually paying attention to the two fabulously dressed octogenarians in the restaurant who are laughing loudly, wearing jaunty outfits and having a better time than anyone else.

Trite though it sounds, I think it's about confidence. In her own more understated way, Ann also busts out some pretty sexy outfits in the evenings – nobody wears a black shift dress like she does. She has a next-level attractiveness that would be impossible in a young person. It's based on her imperiousness as much as anything physical.

There comes a time when there is no point trying to look younger, or smaller, or anything other than you are. You don't have the energy to hold your stomach in or squeeze into jeans half a size too small. And so it becomes about what it should have been all along – comfort, fun, maybe a bit of self-expression.

Establishing the confidence of Ann and the exuberance of Nan and Rose is definitely something I aspire to. From now on, I want to get a head start and try my best to feel like that already.

I start saying things like 'yeah, the purple top with the sparkly bit on the neckline really *does* look cool with the white trousers' and make sure I tell them they look nice, as it's very well deserved. They do and I'm glad. I thought it didn't matter but it really, really does.

December 1947

When partition happened, the family didn't literally have to flee overnight: partition happened in August and they left in December. They had to leave, but they had choices due to Chum being in the Army Medical Corps: there were boats going to Australia, Canada or the UK. They only chose the UK because Chum's father owned a house in Manchester (where none of them had ever been, of course). He sent a telegram to let them know that the whole family would be coming shortly.

They had not foreseen how violent and dangerous the region would become at this time, amid escalating tensions between the newly divided states of India and Pakistan, and the understandable antipathy towards the British.

My nan was born in Rawalpindi, which after partition was in Pakistan. After the family settled in Pune, further south in India, the children were sent away north to boarding school in the mountains for the majority of the year. Nan's school was in Murree, in the foothills of the Himalayas, over the new border in Pakistan. When partition happened, she was mid-way through the school year.

At the time of partition, the rest of the family were sent from their home in Pune to Deolali, where they would be transported to Bombay to take a boat to the UK. This was a transit camp for British troops who had to leave India, and was known for its unpleasant environment and extreme heat. Incidentally, this is where the term 'going doolally' comes from, as apparently that place was enough to make people go mad. Deolali was in India, but Nan and her eldest sister Clara were over the border, and travelling between the two was fast becoming not only extremely inadvisable but pretty much impossible.

Clara had finished her medical training and was working at Nan's school as the school nurse, so they were together, but somehow they had to get back into India to meet the rest of the family. Their passage on one of the last ships out of India was booked; if they had not arrived in time to make the crossing, they would have been left behind.

Fortunately, my auntie Clara was, without question, the absolute staunchest of all the staunch women in my family. She was eight years older than Nan and they were closer than any sisters I have ever met in my life. I suspect that one of the reasons for this was that Clara literally saved her little sister's life in 1947.

Murree was quite cut-off and there were no trains available. Clara managed to get them a lift in a mail van as far as Rawalpindi, where they were then able to get onto a train to Lahore. This was still within Pakistan, so the next step involved them having to get over the border into India.

They joined a military convoy to take them over the border from Lahore to Delhi. This was unpleasant – three days and pretty much sleepless nights stuck in the back of an army truck – and highly dangerous. Clara wouldn't let Nan look outside, and to distract her from the dead bodies that were piled up by the sides of the roads, she read to her from *True Story* magazine. It specialised in real-life romance stories; Nan can still pretty much recite them from memory, she heard them so many times. She remembers lying down in the back of the truck at night and hearing protestors shouting about freedom for Pakistan and getting the British out, explosions ringing in her ears.

The truck was being driven by Indian soldiers who looked after them, but would have been in great danger had they known they were harbouring British girls in the back. People attempting to travel from India to Pakistan, and vice versa, were being slaughtered indiscriminately. Getting over the border was, as Nan puts it, 'mildly hazardous'.

'I can remember the shouting. All sorts of *patarkas* [firecrackers] going off. It was a horrendous time. People were being killed. Slaughtered. It was quite stressful for us, really. The driver and co-driver would feed us, secretly getting food for us while we had to stay in the back of the truck. We couldn't get out in case we were spotted. Who knows what would have happened if we had. We just had to hope we would make it through and join up with the rest of the family.'

Once they were in New Delhi, they were able to take a

train to Deolali, where the rest of the family were anxiously awaiting news of the two girls. Chum walked back and forth to the railway station every day, hoping they would be on one of the trains. There was no way at this point of even knowing if they had survived. Boats out of India were leaving and time was running out, but they were only leaving if they could all leave together.

'They were even killing people on the trains. We were actually very lucky to make it. Our parents were very worried. So many trains were derailed, people were climbing up and travelling on the roofs. The roofs were covered with people. Everyone was trying to get over the border, both ways. So sad. It was the saddest thing.'

During the train journey, Clara made Nan wear a headscarf and keep her head down. Clara was dark and could just about pass for Indian; my nan was blonde and most definitely could not. By this point, not being spotted was a matter of life and death. Nan was a pretty sheltered and naive sixteen-year-old and didn't fully grasp this, as Clara told her to shut up and kept reading her stories from the same *True Story* magazine.

When they finally arrived in Deolali, Nan can still remember how much Chum cried when he spotted them getting off the train.

'I could cry myself, when I think about it now, so many years later. He put his arms around us, crying, "my girls, my girls."'

On seeing him there waiting for them, Nan remembers feeling overwhelming relief at having reached 'safety', even though they still had to get out of India. The family travelled together from Deolali to Bombay, where they were booked onto one of the boats leaving India for the UK. They stayed in army quarters until they received the signal to leave.

Now the family just had to get out of India, and 'back' to the UK, where none of them had ever set foot in their lives.

Present Day

Before we arrived in India, my nan informed me there would be only one rule for the duration of our trip: none of us is allowed to leave the hotel grounds alone. Being the most mobile of our travelling group, I couldn't help but feel that this was directed largely at me.

Having grown up in India, Nan is visibly at home from the minute we arrive there. However, having been brought up in a little bubble of Britishness behind gates and walls, there are some outdated ideas that became ingrained that she has brought along with her. She was brought up to be respectful and somewhat wary of everything beyond the gates – of the people, the food, the water. Most of the time, I am grateful for her knowledge, but there are times when I suspect her caution to be unnecessary.

Also, I try to tell her that some of the questions that she deems to be essential to our survival may be unhelpful.

'Is it clean here?' she asks in every restaurant we go to. 'Is the kitchen nice and clean?'

'Nan,' I say. 'They're hardly going to tell you it's dirty, are they? You're just offending people.'

'Nonsense, darling. You always have to ask.'

Where we are staying, on the coast outside the small village of Benaulim, is very safe and friendly. As we settle into a routine, I begin exploring by myself.

Immediately outside the front gates of the hotel, there is a little parade of shops and several stalls set up around them. Hardly anybody seems to come out this way – I am surprised at how many of the hotel residents seem to stay permanently within the hotel grounds. They stick by the pool, putting out their towels to secure their favourite spots before breakfast. When I wake up early for my daily yoga class, I can see them trotting across the lawns.

So when I begin venturing outside of the gates, I become something of a curiosity. I guess the shopkeepers don't realize how broke I am: how would they know that my grandmother is funding this luxury hotel stay and I have left behind a house that is literally falling down?

There are two Ayurvedic medicine and massage centres. There's a tiny convenience store, just like a corner shop at home but with far more exotic wares, which boasts a revolving, flashing sign proclaiming it a 'superstore'. This never fails to delight me. There are a couple of restaurants. There are the ubiquitous packs of dogs, milling around and calmly minding their own business.

I am soon on chatting terms with pretty much everyone in this little mini village, and it starts a routine that I keep up daily, when we're in the area. When we go off on outings or travelling around, and I return a couple of days later, all of my local friends wonder where we were. They worry that I'll leave without saying goodbye (or without making some last purchases before I go). They constantly make me promise that I won't go home without remembering them. I duly promise.

'Keep your promise. Look at me. You are my friend. Keep your promise,' they all say.

The women who work on the stalls are very friendly, as are their ridiculously cute children, who hang back shyly and stare at me. I'm sure they must be brought out as some sort of marketing ploy, and it works. The stalls all sell pretty much the exact same things: sarongs, Indian dresses and scarves, bits of jewellery, fridge magnets in the shape of Shiva and Ganesh. That sort of thing.

Of course, on my first outing, I get carried away and buy loads for far too much money. A red kaftan that I barely take off for weeks on end. Random beads, scarves and fridge magnets for all my friends back home. Then I feel guilty whenever I come back and don't do the same every time.

Beyond the stalls, there are two roads. One goes into town, which is a walk that Ann and I do together whenever we feel like a change of scene and stretching our legs. It takes about forty-five minutes or so along dusty busy-ish roads with no pavements, to get into Benaulim. In Benaulim there is a bustle of people and mopeds and various animals, along a few fairy-lit roads. It is small, but at first it is dizzying. Everything just feels so *different*. The colours, the smells, the sounds, the people. It feels like it's all turned up to eleven.

On my first visit, I found myself rooted to the spot and awestruck while everyone else rushed around me, with places to go and things to do. Luckily, a kind breakfast waiter from our hotel spotted me and helped me to find my way.

In the opposite direction from the road into town was a smaller dirt track that looped back around to the beach. Everywhere led to the beach, basically. If you take any road, you would just eventually end up much further along the same beach.

Following the beach road takes you around to the hotel's hidden staff entrance, where there are hundreds of mopeds lined up, the main daily form of transport into work. There are so many of them stacked up, and they all look identical, so I have no idea how anybody identifies their own bike out of the line-up. I occasionally hear music coming from this staff area, or see someone I know and wave on my way past, but I don't want to stop and interrupt their break. Everyone here is so nice, they would be too polite to tell me to go away. That first day, when I got mildly lost in downtown Benaulim, it took me a moment to recognize Jai, our favourite breakfast waiter, when he came to my rescue, as he had his hair spiked up and a tight shiny T-shirt on, instead of the uniform I saw him in every morning. He came rushing over the road without any prompting from me, and I was touched that he would bother to help me on his day off, when he absolutely didn't have to. Honestly, if I were him, I would probably have carried on walking and nobody would ever have been any the wiser.

After about ten minutes, walking around the back of the

hotel leads you down to the beach. As you draw closer to the sea, a row of stalls appears. Not many people walk this way, so the ladies running the stalls get extremely excited at the sight of any pedestrian.

It took me by surprise the first time I walked down there. There were about twelve stalls, similar to the ones outside the hotel gates and selling pretty much identical things: trinkets, jewellery, dresses. This time, when I came into view, I was suddenly surrounded by a crowd of women. They all sat on stools outside their stalls and waited for someone to come into sight. It happened so seldom that it was an exciting occurrence.

'My name is Priya.'

'I'm Pritti. Please come inside and see my shop.'

They all introduced themselves, and often their children. The stalls each had a table at the front and a covered tarpaulin area at the back. They were all clamouring to get you into their shop, and once you were in, it was hard to escape. It quite quickly got scrappy. There was no love lost between these women.

Their competitive sales pitches in every direction rendered me paralysed with indecision.

'Small business,' they eventually said, very pragmatically, on seeing this. 'We all sell the same things. Make a small business for each of us if you can.'

I was delighted at this solution. I felt disproportionately guilty about the dichotomy of being a rich Westerner, but also being not at all rich and trying my best to save money. It's all relative, I guess. I wasn't sure how earning a writer's salary and constantly being in my overdraft compared to everyday life around here.

As I got to know them better, I chatted to some of the women on the stalls about how it worked. They said this had been a very bad year and they were making less money than usual, but I shamefully found myself thinking, well, they wouldn't tell me they were having the best year ever and making masses of cash, would they? They explained to me a complicated system that I didn't really understand, whereby they paid for both their rent and their stock upfront and then had to make it back.

To be fair, I couldn't really see how they made much profit at all, as there was not much passing trade. When things were very quiet, I'd see a few of the women walking up and down the beach with some of their smaller items. A few people would stop and chat to them, but mostly they would be ignored and swatted away and generally treated on about the same level as the beach dogs, possibly slightly worse. However, I did laugh once when I saw someone express a slight interest in a bracelet, whereupon Priya pulled about a dozen similar options from her bra. If I ever said I liked one thing, they would say they'd give me a good price if I bought two. This would always baffle me: 'but I only want one, what will I do with two?'

When we weren't going on excursions elsewhere, I would try to visit every day and buy something from someone. I worked my way down the stalls and would promise to come to the next one the following day.

Back home, I once said to my therapist, 'You know how

dogs have no concept of time and every time you leave them, they just assume it's for ever and you're not coming back? Well, that's how I feel in relationships these days.' We agreed that I've been left, with no apparent warning, enough times for this to be unsurprising.

The reaction from my friends on the stalls seems to be the same – they are convinced this is their last chance to sell me things and I might never come back. They grab my hands and look me soulfully in the eyes.

'Keep your promise. Promise me? You'll come back. Promise?'

After a week or so, I'm gratified that they seem to begin to believe me. Each time I tell them how many days I have left before I go home and they take my word for it that they'll see me again. Every time, I feel a bit sad that the number of days left is depleting. I love my routine here.

So, each day I might buy a ring or an incense holder to take home for friends. I buy my yoga teacher cousin some bells to use in her class. I buy my sister an anklet to use as her 'something blue' at her wedding. Every time I take more money out from the cash machine at the hotel, I keep my fingers crossed that it will let me.

I try to buy things that will be genuinely useful – also I am on a limited budget and it makes me feel embarrassed to be behaving like some kind of benevolent oligarch over here. I buy tiny things but spend a long time sitting outside stalls chatting. Fortunately, nobody seems to find this annoying. I like to think they'd tell me if it was. These women seem quite forthright.

Sylvia (some of the women have Anglicised names that I guess must be variations of their real names, but I'm not sure) introduces me to her daughter, who is thirteen, and tells me how proud she is that her daughter goes to school. Sylvia herself can't read or write. Cheesy to say, but it puts things in perspective.

This Western guilt plus my total inability to haggle means I am a dream customer. So much so, it is confusing to my new friends. I ask how much something is, they tell me a made-up number, I inwardly panic about this and say 'um, OK?'. It's the same sort of voice I used to find myself using with Bad Boyfriend – my automatic reflex when I'm uncomfortable. My good manners have always been a problem for me. In this instance, it seems to cause genuine confusion. Some of the women feel so sorry for me and my naive ways, they start giving me presents. It's lovely but somewhat adds to my awkward guilt feelings. A lot of the stuff they're selling goes for much more in overpriced Brighton hippie shops, so I figure I'm getting a good deal anyway.

One problem is, although it's all a similar selection, some of the stalls do have nicer things than others. When I go inside Sonia's shop, about halfway down the parade of stalls and from the outside identical to the others, I pretty much fall in love.

A lot of the dresses and kaftans I've seen look lovely, but I silently lament that they're in such cheap manmade fabrics. They'd get sweaty and gross in a second, possibly go up in flames, and definitely not survive a spin in the washing machine. If I have learned one thing about myself in thirty-six years – and, let's face it, I've managed to learn very few lessons along the way – it's that I am far too lazy to hand-wash anything, ever.

Anyway, Sonia's stall is different. There are racks of beautiful cotton dresses, the sort I dreamed of bringing home from India. They are perfect, total George Harrison Sixties vibes, which is always a theme I will go for. I want to dance around singing 'My Sweet Lord' with joy at the very sight of them.

'You have such beautiful things in here!' I exclaim.

'Ssh, don't tell the others,' she says.

There is one dress in particular I fall in love with. It's full-length, blue and white cotton, long bell sleeves with bells and tassels. She tells me the price and it's roughly the same as something similar would be from a fancy hippie shop in Brighton.

'Um, OK?' I say.

I decide there and then that I will wear it to my sister's wedding in June, then it somehow doesn't seem like quite such a profligate purchase. I tell Sonia this, thinking she will be pleased.

'This,' she says sternly, 'is a very *high-class* dress. If I sell it to you, you must promise me – *promise* – you will wear it nicely.'

'OK . . .'

She looks at me sceptically. I don't blame her. As I do pretty much every day here, I am wearing ratty old denim shorts and a vest, my hair in the same plait it has been in for a few days, throughout sleep and sea swimming and yoga classes. I have flip-flops on and my feet are decidedly dusty. I think it's a look I pull off pretty well, considering I'm not *actually* a Nineties teenager any more, but Sonia clearly disagrees.

'You must promise me. You wear high heels. Make-up. Do your hair pretty. Not – ' she gestures at my general person, making a most distasteful face – '*this*. Promise me not this.'

'Um, OK.'

She tries to sell me some more dresses but, even though I want them all desperately, I genuinely can't afford to buy anything else. I promise her I will come back when I have more money on me.

She hugs me and whispers to me that I am her best friend. I guess that means I paid far too much for the dress, but I am so happy with both the dress and the positive affirmation that I still consider it a bargain.

As I go to leave, she steps in front of the doorway and physically stops me.

'Wait, wait!'

Whenever anything like this happens, I immediately expect to be murdered or at least robbed. It's shocking how quickly murder always comes into my head as the only logical explanation. Then again, what else can it be? Why won't she let me leave?

I'm carrying my beach bag, an ancient Marc Jacobs canvas shopper, which has seen better days and contains all my worldly possessions. Also, the blue plastic carrier bag Sonia has given me containing my new favourite dress.

She grabs my bag off my shoulder. Oh well, I think – being

robbed is definitely better than being murdered. Swings and roundabouts, you know. She then wrestles the carrier bag out of my sweaty hand and takes that, too. Bit rude that she wants her merchandise back as well as all my cash and passport, but ho hum. I guess I'll just let it slide and not put up a fight. I'm such a coward, when it comes down to it.

Sonia starts taking all of my belongings out of my tatty old canvas bag. Maybe she's going to take the good stuff and ditch the rest. I fear she will be sorely disappointed as she sorts through a soggy swimsuit, a notebook containing all my most embarrassing innermost feelings, my beloved iPod Classic and an old Nirvana T-shirt.

Anyway, Sonia shoves the blue carrier bag down into the bottom of my beach bag and then starts carefully packing my belongings back in over the top of it. She folds my towel and bikini much more neatly than I have ever done in my entire life.

'We can't let the others see,' she whispers to me. 'They will be angry with me if they see you bought a large item here. Small business, small business – remember? When you come back and buy more, it will have to be secret. The others will be angry with me. They will not be nice to Sonia. You are my best friend, remember? Don't tell them.'

This would be kind of funny if it didn't make me want to cry. My buying a dress from one of them and not the others clearly made a bigger difference than I would like to acknowledge.

I assured Sonia that I would keep it quiet. A secret between best friends, we agreed. Before I went home, I think I managed to buy something from everyone. Nan and Rose definitely helped, buying presents for all their respective grandchildren. Ann thought I was insane.

I went back and bought three more dresses (that I couldn't afford) from Sonia before I went home, and hid them way down in the bottom of the bag. She hugged me and gave me some free earrings when I left. Really nice ones as well, that I actually wear. When I took Rose in there to buy gifts before going home, Sonia told Rose that she and I were best friends.

I may be needy, naive and slightly delusional – but I still like to think she didn't say that to just everyone.

December 1947

The family left India on the *Empire Halladale* ship, a journey that took over a month.

Dolly was seven months pregnant (for the *eighth* time, at the age of forty-two) and spent the entire journey ill and confined to the sick bay. They must all have been traumatised by their last days in India, and with no idea what was waiting for them in the strange country on the other side. Still, Nan remembers they were mostly delighted just to have all made it out together.

There were a few families like theirs on the boat, but it was mostly shipping home the demobbed soldiers of the Black Watch regiment, who made up the vast majority of the passenger list. The boat set sail from Bombay, made a stop to pick up more passengers in Karachi, then headed for the UK.

They were on the boat over Christmas and New Year. Rose remembers having Christmas dinner on the ship. She also sneaked out alone to join in the New Year festivities, where her abiding memory is of drunk soldiers racing prams up and down the corridors, and having to hide in a cupboard when they started paying her too much attention. She was a very pretty eighteen-year-old at the time. She never told her mum that one.

Nan spent her time at sea writing short stories and diaries that she intended to send to her English teacher at school back in now-Pakistan, Miss de Renzi, not realizing then that she couldn't – that life didn't exist any more.

When they left, Nan had started her 'Senior Cambridge' course – the equivalent to A-Levels – but had not yet taken her exams. She had been hoping to take up a place at teacher training college in Shimla, which of course was now rendered null and void. She wanted to be an English teacher, and I can imagine she would have been great at it.

She was, of course at that age, also perturbed to have been parted from her first crush, Willy Simpson. She still vividly remembers having her first formal dress for a dance at the Burt Club – white satin, with puffed sleeves and a sash – and dancing with Willy. He was literally the boy next door. His family owned a shoe-making business and were shoemakers to the Maharaja.

His family moved to Canada and he ended up marrying Nan's friend Philomena. She's still a little bit pissed off about it.

'Ha! Willy and Philly,' I pointed out, to try and cheer her up about it.

Even seventy years later, she only laughs grudgingly.

Willy Simpson aside, it's so funny the things we remember.

Nan vividly recalls having marmalade for the first time on that boat. She remembers going through the Suez Canal, and waving at children from the deck, who were watching the boat from the shore. But she says she didn't give much thought to where they were going and what it meant for them as a family. I often think how terrifying it must have been, leaving behind everything they had all ever known.

'I do remember feeling sad about not going to college, and I missed my school and my teachers. But I had my parents and my siblings with me; that was the main thing. Still, it was a confusing time for me. I didn't know what to think, really.'

Most of their possessions, collected over generations of living in India, had to be left behind in their old house. They really had no idea what was awaiting them on the other side. Although they had never been to the UK before, they thought of themselves as entirely, quintessentially 'British'. It did not occur to them that the UK would be very different from India.

Also, they were so used to things going their way, to living a life of privilege, they assumed more of the same was awaiting them on the other side. They were incorrect.

This journey was referred to as 'going home', but when they arrived, it wouldn't really be home in any way. Nobody was prepared for quite how different it would be.

Present Day

In India, I do yoga every day. At home, I wish this were true, but it is not.

I first did yoga circa 2001, when I became obsessed with the idea that I could achieve both Madonna's arms and a nicer, calmer personality in one fell swoop. This sort of life-changing efficiency appealed to me. I did the Geri Halliwell yoga video religiously for a while when I was a student (Ginger was always the Spice Girl I related to the most, due to our similarly fluctuating weight and shared fondness for home dye jobs), but I soon gave up when it failed to change my life or my biceps as instantaneously as I had assumed. In those days, most of the lifestyle changes I attempted – macrobiotic diet, kickboxing, becoming a goth – had a similarly short lifespan.

Over the years, I went through intense phases of hot yoga, ashtanga yoga, bellydancing, meditation classes, ballet barre. None of it stuck until thirty was looming and I decided it was finally time to take myself in hand, once and for all.

There were bad habits that I didn't want to take into my thirties with me.

Miraculously, I really did put my mind to it and it worked. Since then I've run three(ish) times a week, been to a dance class once or twice a week (OK, Zumba, but that doesn't sound as sexy), and done yoga whenever I have the time and inclination in between. Through all the shit that's happened since, one thing I have clung to is my exercise regimen. Even though I'm now a slightly-more-than-social smoker, and even when I could barely stomach solid food, I hauled myself around the park for a feeble run three times a week. Even when it was barely at walking pace, it always made me feel better. The only times I've been a week without running in my thirties were when I had the flu and when I'd just had an enormous tattoo on my ribcage that meant I couldn't wear a sports bra.

Much as I would love to be a Zen creature with Madonna arms, yoga is the one that always falls to the bottom of the list and rarely gets done. In the previous year, I probably went to about half a dozen yoga classes at the local Buddhist Centre and one weekend women's yoga workshop that was just a string of really twee words strung together, sounding like something Jamie Oliver might name a child. I think it was Elemental Woman Inner Cosmic Body Wisdom. Or something a bit like that, anyway.

So, although somewhere along the line I have become an annoying person who talks about how running has improved her mental health, I certainly did not intend to come to India for a yoga holiday. There's something about the idea of 'self-care' that makes me recoil. Leave that to the Instagram babes doing downward dog while promoting a sweatshirt that proclaims 'yay kale!'. Back in the day, I was only ever in it for the promise of abs that somehow never materialised, probably because I would turn up at hot yoga hungover and then get chips on the way home, while wondering why it worked for everyone else but not me. I was over that delusion now. However, it begins to dawn on me that while saying the words 'self-care' automatically makes me roll my eyes, I am probably in need of it. I have the time here, after all. And I'm in India, for goodness' sake.

When I discover there is an open all-abilities yoga class every morning at 7 a.m., I decide to try and go as much as possible. Only if I can be bothered. I do not set my alarm – I'm on holiday, after all – but miraculously, I manage to wake up in time to go to the class every single morning. That might be because we're going to bed pretty early. But also, I soon find that I really, really want to go to yoga every day. And my fears of Insta-ready 'self-care' bollocks turn out to be very much unfounded.

I take to going to sleep with the curtains slightly open every night, so that the light will wake me up in the morning. It cuts a wedge-shape of pure concentrated sunshine onto my camp bed every day, which is delightful to wake up to. Nan sleeps like the dead so I don't have to worry too much about disturbing her. I immediately peek out onto the balcony every day to check out the beach view.

Before I go out every morning, I wake up Ann – as long

as I'm up anyway, she's asked me to act as her early morning alarm call. While I'm at yoga each day, she uses the time to go for a long walk. She often meets me on the way back from my yoga class, where we will walk and chat together.

I quietly clean my teeth and throw on the same Prince T-shirt and ancient grey gym shorts every day. My hair stays in the same plait for pretty much a week at a time. On the walk to the yoga studio – well, it's actually a sort of pavilion with a roof but no walls – I check my messages, to see if there's anything from The Lecturer. The odds of him being responsive are around 50:50 but I give it a go every morning on the way to yoga, just in case.

The Lecturer and I are friends again. Slightly inappropriate, boundary-lacking friends. Every time he does something to make me furious with him, which he has done a lot, I dramatically stop talking to him for a while but then he keeps trying to win me over and invariably says something that really makes me laugh, and I just can't stay cross with him. 'You know I don't speak human' is his constant excuse – he's awkward, I'm just so much better at these things than he is, he says. He flatters me until he's back in my good books every time. However, this time, I hope it might stick. We've become much closer over the past few months. Over Christmas, I spent most of my time half-ignoring my family while texting with him continuously. He's been having a hard time and I have appointed myself chief cheerer-upper. I still find it ridiculously gratifying to amuse him. He is also now officially single.

'I fear I may bore you with sickening pictures of my idyllic holiday. You might want to mute me for the next little while.'

'On the contrary, dear Ellie. Please keep me constantly updated with exactly where you are and what you are doing. Send pictures.'

I don't need to be asked twice. He gets numerous daily updates about every detail of life here, illustrated with artful photos of the yoga shack and me in a bikini.

I've got the drill down when I arrive at the yoga shack: total silence, take off shoes and leave belongings in a pile outside, lie down on mat. I'm pretty much always the first one there; the class always starts late. One morning the teacher was still putting mats down when I arrived. When I tried to help him, he shooed me away and acted slightly offended. After that, I just lie down and keep quiet.

He's not like yoga teachers at home. I never even find out his name. It's quite relaxing, actually. He's not a friendly yoga teacher or, thankfully, in any way a creepy yoga teacher. There is no preamble, no chat. No smiling, really.

At my first class, I didn't realize he was the teacher. He's a very small man wearing the sort of outfit that seems to be common as a uniform in the hotels and restaurants – a baggy cream-coloured cotton shirt and matching trousers.

The class fills up while I lie there. It's a mixed class: an Indian family, some older people, a few bendy Western hippies showing off. The teacher has a loud, forceful voice.

'REEEEELAX,' he says loudly, in the manner of a military command.

We duly relax, as best we can.

'BREATHE. CLOSE YOUR EYES. LIE DOWN. FEET FLAT ON FLOOR. I SAID RELAX. RELAX YOUR ENTIRE BODY.'

Every day it's the same: he starts off chanting a few *om*s, and everyone joins in. So far, so standard. Then he starts doing some much more complicated chanting that nobody can keep up with, so we all awkwardly tail off mid-*om shanti* while he chants by himself. He has a beautiful voice. He seems to prefer it when other people don't join in.

'OPEN YOUR EYES WITH A SMILE,' he barks when he's finished.

Every time, I smile at him ostentatiously to show I'm obeying. He never smiles back. Then it's straight down to business. It's much more athletic yoga than I've ever done before. We swoop our arms around in windmills and he tells us to GO FASTER. We sit with the soles of our feet together and have to push the insides of our knee joints up and down with our hands as quickly as we can for thirty seconds. When I later tell my yoga-teacher cousin about this, she is appalled. As the days go by, I'm convinced I can push my knees closer to the floor, but she assures me that this would be impossible. Apparently this motion is governed by the depth of our hip sockets rather than dexterity, and really not something that should be forced.

When we do back bends, I am always in awe. He can bend himself so far backwards that he is literally folded in half. It's really quite a sight to behold. I try and bend at such an angle so that I can watch him throughout.

'BEND MAXIMUM,' he shouts from this *Exorcist*-like

position, his head around the back of his ankles. 'MAXIMUM. ENTIRE BODY.'

When he walks around the room to make adjustments, it generally involves him pressing down on my joints, pushing hard on my back, and contorting me into slightly unnatural poses that I would have said were impossible. It feels quite nice. I like the attention.

When we 'relax' at the end of the class, we lie on the ground while he instructs us to RELAX. RELAX YOUR ENTIRE BODY. He recites every body part that we should be RELAXING, loudly. At the end he always says 'thank you', not *namaste* like they always do at yoga classes in London and Brighton. The irony of this always amuses me so much that I genuinely 'open my eyes with a smile', as instructed.

I see surprisingly few people come back to this class twice. I hear some hipster girls talking about it on the beach, saying 'oh no, I'm definitely not going, I've heard it's *awful*'. This makes me, by default, something of a teacher's pet, not that the teacher ever acknowledges me. A week or so in, and I'm positioning myself front and centre when I arrive early every day. I have never done this at a yoga class – or any kind of class, or any classroom I've ever set foot in – in my life.

Once, an American man asks me outside after the class whether yoga is always supposed to be this hard. I smile knowingly, even though I'm not really sure. I don't see him at the class again.

I'm not sure whether I have RELAXED MY ENTIRE BODY, but I always come out feeling fantastic. I guess it's simply because I'm doing an hour of exercise every day at the exact same time I'm usually getting the Brighton to London train to work. At this time of year back home, that's well before it gets light.

While I'm away I eat curry and rice for every meal and drink beer on the beach on a daily basis, but I have lost weight by the time I go home. For once I am really, really enjoying inhabiting my body.

I tell myself that it's easy to be this healthy when you have this much time. Still, it's really not that simple. I love exercising at home, it's just that sometimes I'm too hungover to enjoy it and it's more of a chore than it is here. Here, practising moderation – something I struggle with massively at home, like so many of us do, particularly those of us whose role in life is to be the 'fun' one – comes naturally. If I go on holiday with my mum or my girlfriends, we start drinking wine at lunchtime and carry on from there. I don't even notice that we're being relatively abstemious here until I realize that – having a cocktail at an appropriate pre-dinner cocktail hour, followed by splitting a couple of beers with Ann over dinner – I don't have a single hangover while we are away. This is definitely the longest I've been without a hangover since my teens, especially on holiday.

I've also pretty much given up smoking – albeit temporarily – because it's just not worth my nan's vocal disapproval. Also, Rose informed me that if she can give up smoking after over fifty years of being on twenty a day, I certainly can – a fact that I can't really argue with.

Moderation seems to be something that comes more

naturally when you get older. Nan and Rose enjoy a drink and don't go crazy on it, which doesn't sound like rocket science, but to me kind of is. Nan does exercises every day, and at home, Rose goes to tai chi class every week. They enjoy their bodies as much as they can at this point. Being old is not for the faint-hearted. The combination of fun and self-care is something that for the over-eighties is not just a nice aspiration, but absolutely vital.

The aches and pains of old age are no joke. When I get run-down, I am prone to kidney infections, which invariably leave me bed-ridden and with such severe back pain that I couldn't get up and go to work if I tried. A while ago, for a few days in a row, Nan said on the phone that she felt under the weather. She continued to drag herself to the shops, to church, to Spanish class, but it was 'a bit of a struggle'. Nan never likes to admit that anything is a struggle, so this was unusual. Of course it was – when she eventually saw her doctor, she had a kidney infection so severe, they wanted to hospitalise her.

'Nan! When I have a kidney infection, I can't even get out of bed. Didn't you realize something was seriously wrong? Didn't your back hurt?'

'Yes, now I think about it. I suppose it did, but not really much worse than usual, with the arthritis. Everything hurts when you get to my age, to be honest, darling. All the time.'

My nan is hard as nails. So is Rose, whose response to the constant arthritic agony in her shoulders is to switch to front-fastening bras. Even Ann, after a lifetime of sport, has had to have a knee replaced. Anyone who makes it to that age is, frankly, heroic. Sometimes I worry I'm not staunch enough to manage old age, if I'm lucky enough to get there. Nan assures me that staunchness increases with age, but I'm certain she was already stauncher than me in her thirties. She was working full-time and bringing up two children by herself. On the other hand, my mobile account is always being suspended because I keep forgetting to pay my bills. I spend hours watching *RuPaul's Drag Race* while drinking wine. Nan's hobby outside of work was to volunteer for the Samaritans.

They say youth is wasted on the young. I don't have that much youth on my side any more, but I've got a lot more than my nan has. Which is why she and Rose are always telling me to make the most of my body, I guess. Having lived in close proximity with them for a while, I get it. They would love to be able to go to yoga class, go running. Also, they would love to get looked at in a bikini. I know that last one because they tell me it constantly.

Present Day

I send a lot of pictures of myself in a bikini to The Lecturer during the course of my time in India. It's all quite wholesome, but I find myself determined to grab any opportunity for him to view me in a sexy light. The existence and casual sharing of these pictures is testament to a big change that has occurred in the last few years, for better or worse.

Past Me: 'I can promise you there will *never* be a naked picture scandal about me. You know why? Because no naked pictures of me will ever exist.'

'Ellie, that's probably also because you're not a celebrity.'

'Yes, but it's the *principle*. Why anybody would ever even take a naked photograph of themselves is beyond me.'

Funny to think I was once so adamant about this sort of thing. It was so easy to say, in that long-ago time when naked picture scandals were first A Thing – what, 2007? I think I still had a BlackBerry, FFS. I had at that point lived with my (very analogue) boyfriend for the past four years. *Of course* no naked pictures of me existed.

I would then go on to tell the *hilarious* story about the time K and I stayed at the Hotel Pelirocco circa 2005, and excitingly, had our room upgraded to the basement suite. Which was basically like a subterranean sex dungeon. Complete with mirrors on the ceiling – suspended above the circular bed – which left me so paralysed with early twenties body-dysmorphic horror, we didn't have sex for the whole of our dirty weekend away.

I turned it into a funny story later on, but actually I spent much of that weekend in the bathroom crying while eating the free retro sweets we'd been given as part of the special sex dungeon package.

My body image at that age was so shaky. My weight fluctuated depending on my mental state – either madly doing exercise videos at 6 a.m. before my unsatisfying temp job and saying I couldn't have a glass of wine because of the 'empty calories', or spending entire weekends eating Pot Noodles and takeaway pizza on the sofa and complaining I felt fat.

Meanwhile, my self-esteem flipped wildly between far too low and far too high. Sometimes I would walk around feeling like hot shit, then I'd be shocked when I saw a picture of myself and realized I didn't actually look anything like Natalie Portman.

These days I have become more solid in my belief that my face suits me and my happiness levels have no correlation with my size. I have become determined not to give a fuck. If anything these days, I have become neurotic about not being neurotic. However, despite all my best efforts, sometimes it still doesn't take much to throw me off.

So, no – not for me. There would *never* be a naked photograph of me in existence. Not in this lifetime, which I thought I had so neatly and cleverly sewn up. So tacky. (And let's not mention that I was so deep in the midst of a phase of cake baking and sitting down at this point, nobody really wanted to see a naked picture of me. Probably including K.)

Fast forward to late summer 2016: a music festival with my friend Alice, in the rain, watching a singer I love.

'Her guitarist is hot,' I said to nobody in particular.

'Urgh, gross!' replied Alice. 'Totally your type.'

And he was. In my dream sex fantasy, all men look like they're made of pipecleaners and could be in the Faces, ideally with shaggy hair, very tight trousers and possibly some sort of addiction problem.

Long story short: when Hot Guitarist then follows you on Instagram and slides into your DMs on *Leonard Cohen's birthday* and you start exchanging witty messages . . . and then you progress onto WhatsApp and you're on your way home a bit drunk on gin, just as – due to the time difference – he's hanging around his apartment in LA and says 'hey, you wanna send me a picture?' . . .

I guess you could sensibly consider the following options:

- You are well into your thirties now and things aren't what they used to be
- You're not particularly adept at taking flattering selfies at the best of times
- Potential cringe factor (high)
- GDPR?

Or instead you could say: yeah, OK, why not?

Basically, I then spent the next couple of months staying in my house, not speaking to any of my actual friends, and exchanging photographs in various states of undress with a sexy rooster-haired musician on a different continent, who had worked on some of my all-time favourite albums.

It was actually fun. Hot LA Guitarist was appreciative and nice, and had a very photogenic penis. I never met him and I doubt I ever will. I knew he would never see me from an unflattering angle, which felt quite reassuring.

For a time, I had a flatteringly lit mirror permanently set up in one corner of my bedroom. A few times we even had FaceTime 'dates'. He once read me his favourite Rimbaud poem via FaceTime while we both drank herbal tea in our respective beds. We agreed we were both intellectuals, you see. Intellectuals who liked to exchange really grubby and potentially embarrassing naked pictures.

When I told Alice – who is younger than me and far more experienced in such matters – she was horrified that I had included both my face and my distinctive tattoos in the pictures.

'You're so naive sometimes, Ells.'

I hadn't even thought of that. Oh well, he's a nice guy and, importantly, he's much more famous than I am so has more to lose. When she then asked me 'fine, but what if his phone gets nicked and some dodgy stranger gets hold of them?', I had no answer to that other than 'fingers crossed, I guess?'.

I suppose eventually the novelty wore off – my photography

skills are rudimentary at best, and there are only so many poses a gal can do in her bedroom mirror while trying to avoid including the dirty laundry basket in the background and sucking in her stomach that furiously. However, I kept all of the pictures. Hot LA Guitarist and I aren't in touch any more. I think of him fondly, as I do all those pictures.

In fact, it was a bit of a revelation. I still take the odd one sometimes, just for myself. If I'm getting out of the bath and putting on my vintage kimono, occasionally I'll think: yes, you are hot and your tits aren't what they used to be but they will never be this good again and, yeah, you have cellulite and stretch marks but you also have a pleasingly solid Kardashian arse and the hair of a mermaid princess.

I think this means I actually feel a lot better about myself now than I did in 2007. I'm also (a bit) less judgey. I'm working on it, anyway.

What I do know for a fact is that the body I have now will be one I think of wistfully when I am eighty-seven. I think back to me at nineteen, sad and skinny and so, so neurotic. I want to give that girl a hug and tell her to eat a burger and drink some wine and maybe do a yoga class and have sex with more people and generally have a lot more fun. I don't want to look back in another twenty years and feel like that about my comparatively hot thirty-something self.

Now, when I'm feeling old and tired, maybe a bit hungover, holding up my tits in the mirror and marvelling that they ever used to be that high up and I want to cry a little bit, I try my best to think of Nan and Auntie Rose.

Although a level of vanity remains, you can't be self-conscious by the time you reach your late eighties. There's a big difference between the two, an important one.

Auntie Rose sometimes needs help getting into a bra due to her bad shoulder. Nan calls me in to escort her across the fancy wet room floor when she's finishing up in the shower as she's worried she might slip.

This casual senior nudity is not only practical, but also the mark of women who no longer give a fuck, in the best possible way. They want to look as nice as they can, hence the endless outfit debates, but they're mostly just pleased about the things they can still do with their bodies. My nan often tells me, while she's doing her morning exercises, that she can still touch her toes, as if I might have forgotten since yesterday. But if I were her I'd probably mention it a lot too. It's awesome.

They take delight in my young(er) body, constantly telling me I've got a great figure and to make the most of it. Their eyesight isn't what it once was, so that might be why, but I choose to believe them.

'Ooh, do you think I could get away with one of those?' Rose asks one evening, as I'm putting on a vintage jumpsuit to wear out for dinner.

'Yes, absolutely,' I tell her. 'Do it. Just don't wait until you're desperate before you go to the loo when you're wearing one. That's my only advice.'

'Oh, yes. Especially at my age. Good point.'

I'm pleased on the rare occasions when the advice can go both ways, and I think they are too.

Present Day

Once I've done my yoga and everyone else manages to get dressed, breakfast becomes the cornerstone of our routine. Not just the most important meal of the day, but a daily highlight in all sorts of ways.

Heading down to the hotel restaurant, our favourite tables are the ones outside – set up on the lawn, with cane furniture and billowing white umbrellas. The outside tables are limited and hotly sought after, but we soon get the breakfast staff onside to save one for us every day, even though we never surface before ten o'clock.

This is the power of my grandmother and her sisters. Nan quickly becomes legendary around the hotel and the entire surrounding area; it's like being in a celebrity's entourage – the celebrity being *the white woman who speaks Urdu*. People can scarcely believe it when she starts chatting away, particularly as she is very fair-skinned and blonde. It's incredibly cool to watch.

I must admit, at first I was worried. After all, it doesn't

take a great deal of knowledge to put it all together: a woman of her age, visibly Western but speaking Urdu. Surely that's got to be the product of some problematic history. Whenever people ask her how she possibly speaks the language, she explains that she lived here until she was sixteen and went to school here. It can't be too difficult to do the maths. However, people are without exception friendly and enthusiastic. I don't think they are hiding any animosity, or if they are, they're doing a brilliant job. This may be due to my nan's personality. Especially, but not exclusively, when she's speaking Urdu, she delights people.

In no time, everybody knows Dot and Rose. It takes an age to get as far as the breakfast table every day, because they have to do their rounds and chat to everyone. Ann and I are just supporting characters, while they are like a couple of minor Royals in Capri pants and floral blouses, waving regally and addressing their public. This is a combination of fellow residents and the staff – our favourite breakfast waiter is Jai, who came to my rescue on my first dizzying trip into Benaulim. We learn that he has recently got married and is apparently a state champion wrestler. He is also very patient with us, which is fortunate, because we have a lot of very specific requirements.

Nan is obsessed with her coffee being very hot – *garam* – and Rose invariably requests so much extra butter (the butter is served in individual curlicued pats in tiny frozen dishes so that it doesn't melt), that they nickname her *Memsaab Makani*, literally Madame Butter. Very *Last Tango in Paris*.

I am extremely bad at asking for what I want, even in

places such as a restaurant, where it is their function to bring me what I want. If my food is cold and disgusting, I will say it's fine. If the waiter looks busy, I will eat dry toast rather than cause the hassle of asking for extra butter. As I watch Rose politely beckon the waiter over again and then accessorise her thanks with a wink, I try my best to take note.

Although I would be hard-pressed to put this into action, because the food is so delicious it's bordering on ridiculous. Without fail, I keep up my routine of curry for every single meal, mostly dosa and puri, which involve excellent combinations of heavy fried pancake and spicy curry. I also develop an unexpected taste for upma, a thick, dry savoury porridge, which is worryingly easy to eat by the enormous repeated bowlful.

Between all the fetching and carrying I've been doing, plus the daily morning yoga routine, I always eat my breakfast with an air of smug serenity in the knowledge that I have truly earned it.

Sitting outside in the morning to eat our breakfast is a treat; the grounds are beautiful and the glimpses of wildlife never fail to delight us. While we eat out in the sunshine, we always see a few white egrets, which seem to be everywhere. They have long twiggy legs and pretty faces, basically like a load of teenage models dotted around the gardens. My nan loves them, callling them *chotur moti* ('little pearl'). However, not enough to get close to them – she has a horror of proximity with Indian wildlife of any kind. If even these ridiculous birds flap too close, she reminds me that I haven't had my rabies shots and to be careful.

So, most days I get told off for feeding the skinny cats that appear out of the bushes every day at breakfast time. There's one white and ginger puss that comes and sits on my lap some days. An English woman about my age who is on holiday with her mother has a slightly passive-aggressive go at me one morning – apparently she has been coming to this hotel every year for ten years and the cat always sits on *her* lap at breakfast. I'd be annoyed too if I were her – everyone wants to be a cat's favourite – but I don't feel bad enough to give up the cat, and I continue to sneak it bits of bacon every morning while it purrs on my knee in the sunshine.

In fact, I should probably try and make friends with this woman – I guess we're a similar age and we appear to be the only people here who are in a slightly similar boat. However, she's a bit scary, so I just smile vaguely and escape as quickly as possible. We overhear her and her mother arguing most mornings ('you're always criticising me, why do you have to look at me like that all the time?'). Well, I say 'arguing', but it mostly seems to be just her shouting while her mother sits and eats her cornflakes in silence. Then the daughter goes outside to stomp about and angrily smoke fags for a while. I comfort myself with the knowledge that at least somebody is even more of an overgrown teenager than I am.

Our very favourite person at breakfast is The Crow Man. We envy The Crow Man. Ann and I both agree that we would like to have his life. His entire job involves patrolling slowly up and down the upper balcony of the restaurant, waving a flag to scare away the crows. He is a walking scarecrow. His job function is, in fact, vital. The crows here are savage, much more intimidating than the wild dogs. You can't leave a scrap of food lying around, or a huge gang of crows (literally, a murder of crows!) will descend instantaneously and decimate it, like evil creatures out of *The Wizard of Oz* or something. Oh, or that Alfred Hitchcock film, I guess.

The Crow Man never, ever looks stressed. I become slightly obsessed with him. I would love to know what's going on in his head while he patrols up and down that balcony for three and a half hours every morning, always at the exact same slow, steady pace. I wonder if the flag is heavy.

His face is impassive. I wave to him every morning and he does not react. I imagine he must have a rich inner life. He must be thinking very, very deep thoughts while he is in this slow, repetitive perpetual motion. It's almost biblical. Perhaps he is engaged is some form of transcendental meditation, or even a Jedi mind trick.

I've decided we all definitely have something to learn from The Crow Man.

January 1948

The *Empire Halladale* arrived in Glasgow on 4 January. I asked Nan how she felt, arriving in this brand-new country with no idea of what to expect there.

'Cold,' she says. 'It was *so cold*. I could not believe it. None of us had coats, stockings, winter shoes . . . Nothing. I cried when we arrived and it wasn't just because I was homesick and confused – I think I was also crying because I was bloody freezing. I'd never experienced anything like it.'

She remembers clearly that she was wearing a little red cotton jacket, pleated skirt, short-sleeved blouse and sandals with ankle socks. It was 3.30 p.m.; it was already dark, as well as cold and foggy. There was a Pathé film crew waiting for their arrival in Scotland, recording the return of the Black Watch regiment. However, the excitement was short-lived.

The plan had been to take a train directly from Glasgow to Manchester, where Chum's father owned a big house. However, they received a telegram on arrival to let them know that Chum's stepmother had in fact sold the house and there was no room for them anywhere else. In one fell swoop, they were homeless refugees. And, along with the five children of varying ages, let's not forget that Dolly was eight months pregnant at the time.

I had no idea of any of this when Dolly and Chum were still alive. I wish I could talk to them about it. My nan is very positive and optimistic by nature, and remembers it through the eyes of a very sheltered sixteen-year-old. Rose, more the realist, just remembers thinking Glasgow was shit. (Sorry, Glasgow. You're one of my favourite cities. I think it was just the culture shock.) She wanted to go home. However, there was no home to go to. There was – somewhat under-standably – not much sympathy for them, either. The feeling at home for the 'returnees' from India was less than friendly. The perception was that they had been living it up, while those back home had endured the Blitz and rationing. And it was true.

'We'd been over there living off the fat of the land,' as my nan put it.

However justified this perception may have been, it did not help with the fact that the family were now homeless, with all of their worldly possessions left behind on a different faraway continent.

Fortunately, as Chum had been in the army, they were able to receive help with temporary accommodation, and they were put up in a hostel outside Glasgow, in Bridge of Weir. They would end up living there for the next eight months. Not only was it grey, cold and drab compared to India, but rationing was still in force – which they hadn't had to think about while they'd been living it up in the last days of the British Raj.

Samuel, the youngest child, was born in Scotland in February, delivered by Clara. She found work using her nursing training and Chum found a job working in a children's home. Like many newcomers to the country today, they found that their skills and experience weren't much use and jobs were hard to come by. They had to do whatever they could.

Nan and Rose, both being of working age, were put to work at the local cotton mill. They all had to muck in.

They stood out a mile when they turned up in their best dresses for their first day at work. It was as if they had come from a different planet, not just a different continent. Fortunately, they were *so* different that everyone there took pity on them. The girls there, who Rose describes diplomatically as 'a little bit rough', found them funny and stuck up for them. Nan and Rose in turn were in a state of utter shock – they had never heard anyone swear until they met the Scottish girls at the mill.

'I'd never heard the F-word before,' Nan said. 'They used to talk about sex. It was a total re-education. Although it might be for the best that I couldn't understand much of what they were saying. I just kept having to say "pardon?"'

Not only did they look and speak differently, but Nan and Rose were useless when it came to work. They had never so much as made a cup of tea, it was brought to them by the servants. Dolly, at the age of forty-two, had never cooked a meal in her life.

They say you can't teach an old dog new tricks, but Dolly had to learn pretty much everything – cooking, cleaning, doing the laundry – from scratch. I am in awe of the staunchness that was required. I'm younger now than she was then, and I wonder how successfully I would fare in similar circumstances. She had brought with her a book of Indian recipes that she had noted down by hand from the cook's instructions, and she taught herself how to make them – where other families at that time would have Sunday roasts, she always made a Sunday curry. Her recipe book also contained a lot of information that was no longer useful to her: how to run a vast Indian household, with tips on how to manage the staff and host formal colonial-style events.

Their circumstances had changed so dramatically, in such a short space of time, but they adapted. I never heard them complain, and my nan doesn't even remember any of them doing so at the time. Mostly, she says, they were grateful.

'We were always so happy together. We were joyful. My parents were selfless people; it's the way families were in India, how Indian families still are. We had each other and we were so close. We shared everything. That's why us siblings still all get on so well. We're all so different, but we are never critical or tell each other what to do. We love each other unconditionally, there's no doubt about it. We got that from our parents. They had so much love in their hearts for people. My mother was also a very high-principled woman. I hope I am too.'

Obviously the whole experience was a total culture shock for them. And, in spite of their best attempts to get on with it, they were unquestionably affected by what had happened during those last days in India. Nan remembers seeing a group of people running down the street one day in Bridge of Weir, and how she turned to Rose in utter panic. They instantly assumed they must be running from some terrible disaster, and they joined in as fast as they could. Turned out they were running for the bus.

'I will never forget that as long as I live. There's us tearing down Bridge of Weir high street . . . When we moved there, we didn't have a clue – the first time we went to the sweet shop, they asked for our ration coupons. We didn't even know what they were.' However, Nan is always at pains to point out that, while their experience was unusual, times were hard everywhere during and after the war. She often says being in London during the Blitz would have been far worse.

In the mill, no matter how many times she was shown, Nan couldn't even get as far as working out how to thread the machine by herself. She managed to last working there for a few months, but this was mostly achieved only through charming people into feeling sorry for her.

Rose, on the other hand, didn't even last that long. The most independent of the sisters – and, as we would say in modern parlance 'a total badass' – she immediately went 'fuck this' and took a train by herself to London, deciding that she might as well try her luck and see what happened.

Present Day

Nan credits a great deal of her staunchness to 'values'. She takes the concept of 'values' very seriously. Much of this is based on the family values for which she attributes her ability to assimilate into a foreign culture under adverse circumstances – no matter how bad things got, the family had each other and were grateful to be together. I'm sure this is at least in part why we continue to be such a close family to this day.

Nan also includes, under the umbrella of 'values', her religious beliefs. She reckons that's what has got her through a life that hasn't always been easy: basically, blind faith. She feels sorry for me that I don't have this.

Every evening when we're going to bed, I somehow forget about Nan's praying ritual. I'll be pottering about and chatting to her – brushing my teeth, plugging in my phone and optimistically checking for any messages from The Lecturer, generally preparing to get into my camp bed for the night (for please let us not forget the camp bed).

'Nan, shall I switch off the light?' I'll ask eventually.

She does not reply, and when I look over to her side of the room, I see that she is sitting bolt upright in bed in her nightie, her hands folded and her lips silently moving. About five minutes later, she will reply.

'Sorry, my darling. I was saying my prayers. Good night and God bless you. Love you.'

I find it comforting to know that I am included in my nan's prayers every night. I know this because she often tells me that she prays for me. Dolly used to pray for everyone in the family by name every night, and now Nan has taken on the mantle and does the same. Given the size of our family, it's not a small undertaking. I may not have faith, but I like the idea of continuing this tradition somehow. I guess I need to find my own version of it.

My nan's religious faith is one of the things I find truly fascinating about her. It's fascinating because it's so surprising. If it weren't for the fact that she's always saying 'God bless you' and occasionally namedrops 'the good Lord', you totally wouldn't have her down as a religious person. I'm not sure exactly what a religious person is supposed to be like, as I don't really know any others, but I can only assume it's generally someone who's a lot less fun and more judgey than my nan. She likes a gin and laughs at my dick jokes, even when she pretends to disapprove. As far as nans go, she's definitely on the rad side.

If anything, I envy her faith. I really do. She has this trust in the universe that everything is going to be OK, which I just do not have. I wish I did. I don't know if I believe everything is going to be OK, which is a bit depressing. I definitely don't believe everything happens for a reason, or that people are essentially good. If I believe one thing, it's that you can never completely know or trust another person. Ever. My nan genuinely believes that 'the good Lord' is totally looking out for her. She feels like she can count on it, and goes about her life accordingly.

If I did have faith, which I do not, I think I'd probably be embarrassed about it. I wouldn't admit it out loud. I like to sort of semi-believe in things that I don't really believe in, that I can laugh at. I am from the generation where everything must be ironic, for whom sincerity or – God forbid – earnestness is embarrassing. At school, you had to pretend to be nonchalant about everything or people would laugh at you, and I have never really grown out of that.

It's why I like doing things that are *so* ridiculously woowoo, there is no option but to laugh at them myself first. I keep crystals all over the house. I wear a million good luck charms – you can generally make a pretty educated guess at how depressed/disturbed I currently am by how many talismanic charms I am carrying about my person at any one time. I live off lentils and Marmite spaghetti, yet I think nothing of paying people vast amounts of money to open my chakras and cleanse my energy and, basically, tell me everything is going to be OK when I don't believe it myself. My house is a tip because I don't have time to clean it; I say I can't afford a cleaner, but I do have a shaman. Sometimes I know my own priorities are fucked. I don't even know if I believe in any of these things. Yet at the same time I don't care. I tell myself it's like therapy or massage or whatever – it's just getting to be self-indulgent for an hour, which is always nice. But this doesn't really explain why I still go to the fortune-teller even when I cut my own fringe with the kitchen scissors because apparently I can't afford a professional haircut.

Maybe I do believe in these things, but I'm just too embarrassed to admit it out loud. At school, we used to make up fake band names in order to catch out girls we thought were too 'try-hard' or jumping on a bandwagon: 'hey, have you heard the new single by the Dustbin Lid Spaceship Horses? It's psychedelic . . . Ha ha, no, you haven't – I just made it up. You're such a try-hard.' I still live in fear of this.

Or, even worse, that time I had a crush on a nice boy called Tony because he had long hair in a ponytail. He was a couple of years older and so I didn't realize he was considered uncool in his year. The ponytail was just a red herring and he was boring and didn't like anything cool at all. I only found this out after I kissed him, and then everyone thought it was hilarious and I had to pretend I never even liked him. I still feel bad about that, but I think he got married to someone else so he's probably over it these days.

My nan is utterly unembarrassed about her faith, which is both baffling and awe-inspiring to me. I don't know how she does it. No offence to her or to organized religion, but I'd feel so cringey about that. Nan rarely feels cringey about anything, which is a form of staunchness I totally aspire to.

For my unrelentingly ironic, Alanis Morissette generation, this is unthinkable. Earnestness is our kryptonite. Sometimes

being constantly ironic is exhausting, not to mention dispiriting. I guess if I had to sum up my religious convictions, it
would be some combination of:

- Burning sage in the kitchen to get rid of the spirit of
  ex-boyfriends, while drinking wine
- Thinking a new shampoo is going to change not only my
  hair but my life
- The generous and joyous spirit of the rebooted *Queer Eye*
- Joan Didion
- Cher
- The way I feel in my chest when the *na na na*s really kick
  in towards the end of 'Hey Jude'.

While I'm doing yoga every day, Nan talks about wanting
to go to a service at the village church in Benaulim. It's a
huge, modern white building that was built surprisingly
recently. It's one of the main local landmarks and everyone
we speak to is very proud of it. However, we also learn that
the service starts every morning at six o'clock. The people
here are obviously more dedicated than those at home. I don't
really know anyone who goes to church, but I definitely know
even fewer people who would go to church at six in the
morning. They might not even make it to a really hipster
exercise class at that sort of hour.

We visit a lot of churches over the course of our trip, but
we never make it to a service. I tell Nan that she doesn't
need to worry. I think she probably gets a free pass for
skipping church for a few weeks. She is unfailingly kind to

everyone we meet, and endlessly patient with me, who can be moody and annoying to the point of total ungodliness.

So, although she does not pay him an official visit the whole time we are in India, I am pretty sure that her god will not hold it against her.

November 2017

During the months before going away, as well as seeing my therapist for an hour every Wednesday, I have been having another kind of counselling with a friend of mine.

My friend Rana is a shaman. I first went to see her when I was at my lowest ebb, a few months after Stepdad disappeared, when I was still incapable of functioning as a normal human. She knew nothing about my situation (she had asked me not to tell her in advance), but she put her hands on my chest and wept. She said she could hear me saying 'how could he? how could he?', repeatedly. It wasn't a boyfriend, she said – it was a different kind of male figure.

My mum went to see her too. At the time, Mum believed her luck had run out; she felt as though someone had put a curse on her. We both left Rana feeling better than we had before.

Rana and I stayed in touch over the years and I went to see her every so often. The first time, she was living in a flat above a Subway in Brighton, with a tiny kitten she had recently adopted, who stayed curled up by my side the whole time I lay on the floor in her sitting room. She has since moved to the country, where she has many animals and a special practice room.

I would usually visit Rana in the midst of a crisis. Just being in her presence made me feel better, always. She's that sort of a person. She's much prettier than I ever imagined a shaman would be, and surprisingly down to earth – the perfect combination of ethereal and ordinary. She's special, but straight-talking; there's magic to her, but no bullshit. She's only a couple of years older than me; she has the face of an old-school film star, with a lilting Welsh accent and intricate hand tattoos.

When K and I were in the midst of breaking up, she told me that my mum, K and I were siblings in a past life. I was the youngest and I had died, when I was still a child. K and my mum had tried to look after me, but they couldn't and they were tormented by it; that's why they were still both here, trying their best to look after me. I don't know why this didn't sound completely bonkers but it didn't. For some reason, it instantly rang true.

I rang my mum to tell her about this revelation.

'Mum? Rana said you, me and K were siblings in a past life.'

'I know. I was the eldest, obviously.'

'That's exactly what she said!'

'Shit. I have no idea where that came from. It just came out of my mouth.'

I went to see Rana again when I was in the midst of the ensuing rebound situation.

'Use contraception,' was her surprisingly practical advice. 'I'm saying that not as a shaman but as your friend. Be careful right now. To quote the great RuPaul: don't fuck it up.'

A few years later, not long after the Bad Boyfriend experience, Rana sent me an email out of the blue. She was studying to become a shamanic teacher, learning how to guide people to do their own shamanic journeys. She needed students to practise on, for free – would I be interested?

As these things always are with Rana, it was perfect timing. So, every week for six weeks, she came round to my house. Her presence made me feel immediately better. We would drink camomile tea and then I would lie on the floor in my spare room and learn how to do my own shamanic journeying.

This involved lying down on the carpet, wearing a blindfold and headphones, with tribal drumming playing in my ears. I had to think of an 'access point' in order to travel to 'upper' or 'lower world'. According to the 'shamanic map', we live in middle world (it's all very *Lord of the Rings*) and can travel to the upper and lower world, in order to explore and ask spirit guides a question. The access point I visualized was very prosaic: a tree I like in the park at the end of my road.

The first time, nothing happened.

'Your energy is stuck because *he's* still here,' she told me. I knew exactly who she meant.

'I can practically see him in the room. His energy is all over your space. I can feel his anger.'

She cleanses my house and me along with it. We burn palo santo (sacred wood from South America). She has satisfyingly chunky maraca-like instruments that make the loudest rattle known to human ears, used to break up energy. She rattles them all over the place. She draws his energy out of me, like she's sucking it through a straw from a point in the middle of my forehead.

When she's finished, I feel like I've lost about half of my body weight. I can feel the bad vibes leave me. At that instant, we both jump as we hear a sharp smashing sound. It sounds like one of the upstairs windows has broken. Without exchanging a word, we both run around the house in a panic, trying to find what it was that made such an alarming noise.

We look at each other and burst out laughing. Did we both imagine it? The windows are all intact. Nothing is visibly broken.

It's only on closer inspection that I realize a delicate glass vase in my bathroom fell into the bath – the bathtub is full of minuscule, glittering shards that take days to fully disappear. Even after I sweep up several times, I keep finding tiny slivers.

I say 'fell', but in reality that vase must have somehow leapt. It had been there for years, in exactly the same place. It was not anywhere near the edge of the window ledge it was sitting on.

I still can't explain it, but the following week Rana came over again and I lay down on the floor with my blindfold and my headphones on, and I did a shamanic journey so effortlessly it was like I'd been slipping between dimensions all my life.

Rana recorded all of our sessions, while I narrated them out loud. ('I'm walking down the road, past the garage, past Natalie's house and the pub, over the road and into the park . . . I can feel the grass under my feet and I'm going to climb up my tree now . . .') I was glad she did, because afterwards I would have no recollection of the details. It would feel like no time at all had passed, but also like I had somehow been on an epic hero's odyssey.

I went under the earth and above the sky. I swam in a silver lake and climbed jagged mountains that looked like zigzags a child had drawn. I crawled through moss and into caves. I explored a crystal city. I walked through fields and I could feel my feet getting wet.

I felt cold and I felt hot. I tunnelled through the earth with my bare hands and when I came back I was genuinely surprised my fingernails were not ragged and filthy. A hare told me to be patient. I chased a girl through a forest before I realized she was me as a child.

The thing is with all this, which Rana says herself: it doesn't matter whether you believe in any of it at all, as long as it makes you feel better. It *was* making me feel better. Just being around Rana made me feel better, and I felt like maybe she was giving me a little bit of her magic. God knows I'd needed it. It made me feel stronger.

In our last session together, she asked me to have a think in advance about a question I wanted to ask. I would write my intention down, repeat it out loud three times, and then

I would journey to find a spirit guide who I could ask my question. This culmination of all our work felt important; I had to make it count.

I naturally assumed my question would be about boys. I thought about the Bad Boyfriend, and a bit wistfully of The Lecturer, on whom I was pinning far too many hopes. Instead, I found myself asking about my one true love. The one who had been there all along, right under my nose, just like in all the best romantic stories.

I asked about writing.

I love writing – always have, always will – but I had been struggling. I didn't want to write another book if I didn't have something to say. I didn't want to keep writing the same sort of thing over and over again, but I didn't know what to do next. I had spent months slaving over a difficult three-quarters of a novel before deciding it was useless and abandoning it. I was out of ideas.

All I knew was I had to do something that truly excited me. There were more than enough books in the world already – the world certainly didn't need mine just for the sake of it. Unless I had a great idea that really spoke to me, I wondered if I should consider giving up. But I knew I really, really didn't want to. I hoped it wouldn't come to that. And yet no ideas would come.

Maybe shamanic journeying would help inspiration to strike me, which would be really good timing, because the trip to India was coming up in just a few weeks so I'd have a month off. If I could hit on a good idea before then, I could spend my holiday writing, using the time to get productive.

'What is my true purpose in writing?' I asked.

The answers never come in words. That would be too easy. They're not always as dramatic as inexplicably smashed glass, either. Sometimes they come to me like watching a film on a flickering screen. Once I felt a hand pressing on my chest and felt like I was having a vision, like it was being pushed into me. Sometimes it was just a feeling, or a flash of something that made no sense at the time, like a lost puzzle piece that later falls into place.

In this final journey, I could see myself walking on the edge of the coast, the sea to one side of me. I could feel the sun on my back, my eyelids full of red and heat. I felt peaceful, like I didn't need to hurry.

'It's all already there,' a voice said to me. 'You just need to write it down. You'll know what to do.'

It's only when I'm taking one of my long walks on the beach by myself, the Arabian Sea to one side of me, that I realize I have seen this exact scene before. And I know what to do.

Present Day

'Nan and RJ: A Love Story'. I'm pretty sure that if and when they make a heart-warming British rom-com about our jolly, intergenerational trip to India, that's what it will be called.

All of my friendships with the local people I meet on this trip pale into total insignificance compared to Nan and RJ.

Nan becomes friends with everyone. Her ability to speak fluent Urdu and to chat to every human being she encounters has an effect that is something like magic. She seems to attract people wherever she goes, and soon knows their entire life stories.

She can often be heard saying sentences that I would not dream of, such as:

- I'm going round to have dinner with that nice family who run the corner shop.
- I'm going out for lunch with that taxi driver who took me into town the other day when it was raining.
- That nice girl who lives over the road is coming round

for coffee; you know, her husband's left her and she's bringing the children with her.

Here in India, the breakfast waiters are some of her favourite new friends, as are the buggy drivers. The buggies, we have to admit, have been an actual godsend. You can request one any time, to take you across the vast grounds, from the restaurant to the pool or back to the room. If it's quiet, sometimes we just request a little tour. Ann and I help Nan and Rose to get in, then we perch on the back and hitch a lift along with them. At first I feel mildly guilty about this, as if I should be jogging alongside instead, but then I see quite a lot of guests my age and younger taking them just because they're lazy or drunk, or it's a bit too hot.

RJ, though, he is the one. Her true love on this holiday. The instant chemistry between them is so bizarre, it's quite unsettling. RJ is the assistant reception manager. I guess he is in his twenties. He's skinny and quite nice-looking in a very preppy, clean-cut sort of a way. His hair is very, very neat.

At first I think his manner is so obsequious, it makes me vaguely suspicious. However, I am not permitted to say anything remotely critical of RJ, Nan's favourite human being in the Goa area, her sisters and granddaughter included.

His reception desk is behind a glass door that we have to walk past every time we go in and out of our rooms. Every time, without fail, RJ catches sight of us and comes running outside as fast as he can so that he doesn't miss us. Well, he doesn't want to miss Nan. He doesn't appear to give much of a shit about the rest of us.

'Madam, madam!' he cries as he comes trotting out, holding out his arms.

'Oh God, here comes your boyfriend,' Ann and I can be heard to mutter.

Nan and RJ then embrace at length, as if they are recently reunited long-lost relatives. Then she keeps her arms around his waist a little longer than I am comfortable with. She grins like a smitten schoolgirl when he is around. They obviously both enjoy this slightly weird interaction, so I'm not sure why it bothers me.

'You're my favourite, RJ!' Nan will say, patting his arm. 'Such a lovely boy.'

'It is you who is my favourite, madam,' he will reply solemnly. 'It is a pleasure to do anything I can for you.'

As we head back to our room, they always crane their necks to wave at each other until we go out of sight, me chuntering about it all the way.

'He's a bit of a creep, Nan.'

'Oh, stop it. He's so sweet, such a lovely boy. I love him.'

'You love him? Really?'

'Shut up.'

We don't really know anything about RJ – including his real name – but Nan says he must be both 'very bright' and 'from a very good family', because he is so well spoken. He does seem ambitious, I'll give him that. I think he seems a bit shifty, but Nan says he's just very formal and professional. Aside from the hugging, I presume.

As the days go on, Nan finds every excuse possible to visit RJ's reception desk. He is unfailingly enthused every time.

Actually, I have to admit that it becomes extremely helpful. I begin to understand the appeal of RJ, when he starts dealing with Nan and Rose's tech support so that I don't have to. Obviously, RJ sorting out their iPhones is far more appealing than boring old me doing it. Good old RJ, I find myself thinking more and more often.

'RJ, darling, would you mind having a look at my iPad in the morning?' Rose asks him late one evening as we are returning from dinner. 'I think I'm having problems receiving emails. I'll come and find you in the office tomorrow.'

Ten minutes later, there is a knock at the door. RJ has finished his shift and explains that he wanted to come by to help before he goes home for the evening. It is about eleven o'clock at night.

'You see, I did not want to wait for the morning. Otherwise, madam, I would not sleep well knowing you were having such difficulties.'

This is so sweet but I, shamefully, have to try my hardest not to burst out laughing. He genuinely would not sleep tonight knowing an old lady is having trouble receiving emails on her iPad.

It's mildly uncomfortable having RJ in the room with us, although thankfully, he refuses my awkward offer of a cup of tea. He fiddles with Rose's iPad for a couple of minutes and solves the problem, to much grateful applause.

'You should find a boyfriend like RJ,' Nan takes to informing me at regular intervals from then on.

'You want me to go out with RJ? I don't think you actually mean that, Nan.'

'Well . . . No, you're right. He's not your type, darling, I know. But someone *caring* like RJ.'

I have to admit, perhaps in her own way she has a point.

Present Day

While I'm away, I find myself thinking quite a lot about my taste in people. Not just in men, although it's true I do have a very specific 'type' that has not always served me well.

I tend to get addicted to people, especially to the ones that don't like me very much. I love having to work hard, to win people over, even though it's exhausting. Even with K, after years of being together, I felt as though I had to be the 'best' girlfriend and entertain him at all times – otherwise, what use was I? Of course, my experiences with Stepdad have shown me that's literally how it works. You will never be worth sticking around for, no matter what you do. This does not stop me from trying. Constantly, unfailingly, like my life depends on it. It's bloody exhausting.

Even here, on this momentous holiday and supposed break from everyday life, my mood can hinge on how quickly The Lecturer replies to my texts and whether he laughs at my jokes. It's a bit embarrassing, but there it is.

It's an ongoing battle and it's impossible ever, truly, to

'win'. Sometimes I wonder what it would take for me to feel better, to relax in the knowledge that I was just enough for someone. It's not a feeling I have ever experienced.

For years – the whole time I was with K – I was vehemently and vocally 'anti-marriage'. If you don't get married, you can't get divorced, I would say to anybody who would listen. And I've seen so much divorce, I absolutely knew I did not ever want to go through that.

I really thought I had it all figured out. It used to drive me mad when people would assume that I was patiently waiting all those years for him to propose – this used to happen a lot, particularly at friends' weddings or thirtieth birthday parties. I was always at pains to point out that it was a mutual decision, if not mostly me – 'I'm just not the marrying type!' I would say airily, hoping it made me sound incredibly cool and a bit mysterious.

It was only when it all went wrong between me and K that I changed my mind. I found myself wondering if we'd got it all wrong, if things might have been different if only we'd got married. After we broke up, I felt like a divorced person (I still do) but without the socially accepted weight of 'A Divorce'. It was just a break-up.

Somehow, perhaps now I've seen how impossible it all is, I find my parents' unfailingly optimistic attitude towards the institution of marriage commendable. They just love being married. Even on the third go, they like to believe it will last for ever this time. It truly is the triumph of hope over experience. It's flawed, but it's kind of beautiful.

I want to try everything. I want to have all the experiences.

I still want to do new things. I've had a few relationships, a couple of them serious. What's still left to try? Being traditional, I guess. Taking the leap and marrying someone.

I now think I would like to have a husband and children, and if I'm going to do that, I really need to get on with it. Yet I still seem to put myself into situations where that is impossible, then complain about it.

My mum is one of those women who men seem to want to marry. Pretty much every boyfriend she has ever had has tried to wife her up. They're always trying to do a marry on her. She's had more marriage proposals than I've had second dates, seriously.

My mum loves being married. So does my dad. They both actively seek out marriage. It has to be marriage.

'You should try it,' my mum says to me.

'Mum, literally nobody has ever asked.'

'I don't believe that's true!'

'No, honestly. I know that's hard for someone like you to believe. Nobody has ever wanted to marry me. Nobody has ever asked.'

'Well, to be fair, you can't knock about with all these cool, unattainable men in bands, or artists or whatever, and then complain they don't want to marry you. Just change your taste in men a bit, and I'm sure lots of them would ask.'

She has a point, but it's not like I could ever bring myself to do that, so it's not very helpful advice. I can't help who I fancy.

I've lived alone for over two years now. I've got used to living on my own. I am just not prepared to compromise.

But that's less scary in your twenties, when you have all the time in the world, much more so when you're thirty-six. I am just not capable of 'settling' for anything less than extraordinary.

In the last few years, though, I haven't really felt strong enough for anything extraordinary. Since everything that happened with Stepdad, and K, I feel like I've never quite got back up to full capacity. I'm like an old iPhone: the battery just won't stay charged.

When you're at a low ebb, the wrong people are drawn to you – they can sniff it out a mile off, they circle like vultures. Since Bad Boyfriend, I've felt like I have been systematically broken down, and I'm still putting myself back together again. So, I've continued to complain that I would like someone to want to marry me, but I haven't had the energy left to really mean it. I'm acutely aware of time ticking, but now I realize – instead of running around and panicking, trying to make everything into *something* – really I've just needed a break.

I feel like now, for the first time in a long while, my energy is truly starting to recharge. Not so long ago, I was still exhausted. I still feel a bit like a one-eyed, battle-scarred cat. These days I'm more suspicious of the world, of people, of men in particular. I've been too scared to be adventurous any more.

I have been complaining to my friends about The Lecturer for what feels like forever – he's an enigma, he's strange and stand-offish, he's so confusing sometimes. But it occurs to me now that maybe that's been part of his appeal. Maybe I didn't really want him to be as madly in love with me and desperate to be my boyfriend as I had automatically assumed. Maybe the fact he always kept me slightly at arm's length was part of what was comforting about it.

Maybe I didn't really want it to come to anything. But maybe now I do. That's really something new to think about.

Present Day

While I'm away, I think a lot about all the relationships in my life. I guess the distance puts things into perspective.

Seeing Nan, Rose and Ann together – laughing, bickering, often singing – makes me miss my sister Katy.

Katy and I, in many ways, are polar opposites. Our faces are similar, but we look like distant relatives from two different eras. She has blue eyes and pale skin and a notably slight figure. She is pretty and neat, where I am messy. She is cautious and quiet; I am, as if it needs to be said, neither of these things.

Mostly, when we were growing up, I think Katy viewed me kind of like E.T. I was an alien living in the house with her – I was friendly and funny, but also an entirely different species. I might have been older, but she was always far, far more sensible.

'I thought you were supposed to be the clever one,' Katy often says, rolling her eyes. However, we love each other fiercely and, as adults, we get on brilliantly – until my mother sets one foot in the room, when we invariably regress and start bickering like idiots.

'Mum, she's *looking* at me!'

'Girls, grow up – you're in your thirties now, for God's sake . . .'

While on the surface the two of us appear to have little in common, we both love spending time together. When everything else in my life is going to shit, I know that I can always go and stay at her house, put on pyjamas and eat a takeaway in front of the telly.

She is secretly hilarious (I like to think of her as a Trojan horse when it comes to comedy, what with her sweet and innocent appearance) and she can make me laugh like nobody else on the face of the planet. She's a solid person, a proper person, and I am so lucky to have a sister like her. I'm admiring of her in so many ways.

In fact – although I have never heard my sister swear, or seen her drunk – she's way more of a badass rebel than I am, in so many ways. She has this core of steel running through her that I just don't. I can talk a big game, but when it comes down to it, I am skinless. In her own quiet way, Katy is much tougher than me or my mum. She's one of those people who can charmingly say no to things and never does anything she doesn't want to do.

When we were growing up, as the eldest, I felt somewhat responsible for both of us – for making sure we made a good impression, for making sure everyone got along. It's funny, my parents would definitely say Katy was the easiest of their daughters, but I am the chronic people-pleaser –

it's just that I usually mess it up under pressure (by getting drunk, falling over, or generally getting things wrong), so nobody realizes that's what I'm trying to do. Katy, when it comes down to it, actually gives far fewer fucks than I do.

Despite being the younger sister, I think Katy is already on the path to one day being a staunch old lady. She's already well on her way there. She's got her shit together.

Katy didn't fancy coming on the trip to India. If anything, in a practical sense, she's even closer to our grandmother than I am. She still lives in our hometown, literally round the corner from Nan, so they see each other most days. They go shopping, or out for coffee together, and at the weekends, Katy and her fiancé help Nan with the gardening. They are a couple of earth angels.

While I ring Nan up and chat to her about nothing for hours on end, she would find it a lot harder to function without Katy. We all would, quite frankly. However, Katy had next to no interest in coming with us on this trip. She hates flying and doesn't particularly even like going into central London. She prefers being at home more than anywhere else, and she has styled her house and garden so immaculately, I probably wouldn't want to leave either if I were her. She loves going shopping and eating in restaurants. She likes a nice holiday as long as it's not too far away – she was the first to admit that she probably would have enjoyed our hotel in India, but she wouldn't have wanted to venture further afield than the pool.

Often on this holiday, I think she'd hate it – she wouldn't

like the food, she would hate people constantly trying to sell her things. She does not enjoy hassle. I miss her, though.

I look at Nan and Rose together, and I marvel at how they have been a constant in each other's lives for so long. They bicker, which is extra hilarious to see in two octogenarians. They still have flashes of ridiculous sibling rivalry over the funniest, most trivial things. They argue about things that happened sixty years ago. They love each other fiercely.

I see them on the beach together, walking slowly now and holding onto each other's hands, as much out of necessity as affection, and it blows my mind how much they have both been through in this life. They have seen so much and they have been there for each other through all of it.

They're old now, and they've schlepped halfway around the world just so that they can go back to where it all started, together. That was so important to them.

I would say I hope Katy and I might get to be that lucky one day – but mostly, I hope we get to be that fucking staunch.

The person I miss most while we're away is my mum. We all wish she could have come with us.

She has a high-powered job and has recently re-married; of course she couldn't come. In fact, for her honeymoon, she and her new husband went travelling around India and saw Nan's old school and the hospital where Auntie Clara worked. My mum has a great affinity with both India and family history; she would love to have come if she could.

I feel her absence a lot of the time. When I hear all the old family stories, I'd love her perspective on it. She is the next step on the ladder of staunchness.

While I could still lie down on the floor and weep when I think of what she has gone through over the past few years, I know there is nobody in the world who can laugh in the face of adversity like my mother can. That's something that runs in the family.

In some ways, I feel we're so close because we grew up together. She was twenty-four when I was born. I guess this wasn't unusually young for the time, but it seems like it to me now. She got pregnant by accident because she had been told it was unlikely she could ever have children. Considering she again accidentally got pregnant with my sister three years later when she had an IUD, I think it's safe to say that the doubts about her fertility were unfounded.

When I think about how close my mum and I are – in age, as much as everything else – it blows my mind a bit. In pictures of the two of us when I was a baby, to me, she looks like a pretty student holding somebody else's baby for a joke.

For a treat as a child, I would ask to look through my mum's photo album of her university days. She and her flatmate Celia (my beloved godmother) were my style icons: smoking cigarettes, having wild parties in their flat and looking like total rock chicks. They lived in a condemned building on Gilbert Street, just off Oxford Street – their local shop was Selfridges Foodhall. The flat was decorated with cigarette packets and the 'Tickets and Trains' sign they had nicked from Bond Street Station. The bathroom plumbing was dodgy, so they had a tin bath that they would fill up in the kitchen.

I would listen to these tales like they were fairy stories. I was furious that she'd chucked out her Seventies dresses and Biba collection. I wanted to be exactly like her.

When I was a teenager, we both loved Prince and The Lemonheads, singing along together in the car to school. We would share clothes and argue over missing lipsticks and earrings. If I was going to a party, I'd get her to do my hair and make-up for me. She's always been so much better at that kind of thing than I am.

When my mum was the age I am now, she had a twelve-year-old and a nine-year-old. Her first marriage had ended and she was about to get married for the second time. The idea of this is unthinkable to me. I look at pictures of her at this time, and I could drown in the vast canyon between us.

It makes me look at myself differently. Dating now is difficult, because I look in the mirror and feel like I'm at the wrong stage. Despite the tattoos and overgrown hair and the leather shorts I still insist upon wearing – at my age, at best, I look like a hot mum. I look like my mum looked when I was twelve. If I had been married for five years and had a couple of small children, I'd probably be the coolest-looking mum in town. However, for a single woman – well, by this point, I can't help but feel that I'm sort of lacking.

Far from looking young for my age, now every one of the last five years shows up on my face – you could balance a pound coin in the frown line between my eyes. If I ever get married, my husband will never have seen my tits at their best, which is a shame.

Every day throws up something more dispiriting that I can't control. A lot of this consists of hair in unexpected and annoying places. I have to start bleaching my new moustache, for the first time in my life, and plucking around my belly button. Staying neurotically on top of the nipple hair is a fucking full-time job. I can't decide if I can be bothered or not. Sometimes I leave it and pretend I'm Frida Kahlo, but then I worry that nobody will ever fancy me again. I've always prided myself on my lack of vanity; now I understand why my mum always rolled her eyes at me and said it's easy not to be vain when you're sixteen, twenty-one, twenty-six, even thirty . . .

We often get mistaken for sisters, which these days I think speaks as much of my ageing as it does her lack of.

What all this really means, though: having a life that is anything at all like my mum's is a closed-off path for me now. The idea of that is over, impossible. It's funny getting to this age and realizing that you are running out of potential.

I feel strangely out of time, here on the beach. I see people wondering what my relationship to the others is. I feel like the child of the group, but then I'll see local mothers with husbands and multiple children, who are clearly at least ten years younger than me. It makes me feel like I don't quite belong anywhere.

When I was a teenager, I assumed I'd be just like my mum

when I grew up. I guessed I'd have babies in my early twenties and be a cool, sexy mum just like her. There have been a lot of relatively early pregnancies in my family and thus a lot of cool, sexy young mums. I thought that was the norm.

It's also meant that I've been incredibly lucky in the time I've had with my family. Just as my mum and I have grown up together, it's given us both years with my nan and even great-grandmother that most people never had. My nan was fifty when I was born; Dolly was alive until I was twenty-one. How many people, at the age of thirty-six, are able to go on holiday with their grandmother? I know how lucky I am.

But I have broken the chain. No matter what I do now and what choices I make, I will never be a cool young mum. The idea of that is weird to me. Even if I do have children, I will be an older mother. I don't really know what one of those looks like, how they are supposed to be.

Still, in my family, we are mistresses of reinvention. My mum's life has never gone the way she thought it would. Not once. In these last few years, I have watched her incredible example as she has had to build everything back up from the ruins unexpectedly left around her.

Sometimes I feel like that's what I'm doing every single day. I couldn't do it without her and the other important women in my life, staunch examples all. While we're in India, I think about this a lot. It's a great privilege to be here with the older generation, but I still miss my mum every day. I'm thirty-six years old, and I miss my mum when I'm not with her. I don't think I will ever outgrow just wanting my mum. I have no idea if that's normal or not.

April 1948

Rose arrived in London by train – alone, at the age of nineteen – when the rest of the family were still in Scotland.

'So courageous,' Nan notes admiringly of her cool big sister. 'Valiant. I don't even know what the word is, really.'

Rose chuckles. 'I suppose it was rather. I didn't really think about it.'

She tells the story like it was no big deal. I have come to the conclusion that we start off brave, then dip in the middle and get scared of everything, then come full circle and start giving fewer fucks when we get older. I hope so, anyway.

Our family had considered themselves to be 'from London' during their Indian years, although they had never been in a city anything like London, and the place would have been overwhelmingly foreign to them.

Nan remembers jitterbugging with a glamorous British soldier at a dance at the Burt Institute in Lahore, not long before they had to leave the country.

'Where are you from?' he asked her.

'London,' she replied, trying to impress him – to this day, she's not entirely sure why she said it. We've all said weird things out of nowhere to try and impress a boy.

'Oh, so am I! Which area of London?'

She was so embarrassed, she excused herself and ran off. She'd had no idea that there were different areas of 'London'.

On the other hand, Rose – always the adventurous older sister – arrived in the big city by herself and quickly managed to sort herself out a job and a flat.

Rose had always been independent. During the war, fresh out of school and still living at home in Pune, she joined the WACI (the Women's Army Corps of India). She learned how to drive a truck, ended up becoming a sergeant and generally had the time of her life. When the war finished, she didn't want to go back to her normal schedule of doing not much.

So, as soon as the war was over, she decided to leave home and move to Bombay. She moved into the YWCA and got herself a job as secretary to the director of British Insulated Callender's Cables Limited.

When Dolly found out about this new job, she travelled to Bombay and paid the director a visit, explaining that she wasn't thrilled about her daughter working for a living, so Rose was only permitted to accept the job if he could person-ally assure her that she would not take public transport to work by herself.

And that's how Rose became the only secretary to have her own personal driver, to ferry her to and from work each day, as well as home for lunch. With her secretarial wages, she was able to afford a private single room at the

YWCA, while most of the other girls shared, and her own personal servant.

Rose has always been an early and excellent example of 'knowing your worth'. When I spend time with her I am often reminded of this – she politely and firmly speaks her mind at all times, with her friends, in restaurants and sometimes to strangers, who she just thinks are not being well mannered. She is staunchly magnificent.

Anyway, Rose had a great time being newly independent in Bombay, during an era when young women didn't really live independently. She certainly did. She spent her weekends going to dances, and hanging out with boys at the Bombay Flying Club and the Breach Candy Club. The Breach Candy Club was a 'Europeans-only' club founded in the nineteenth century for swimming and sunbathing in an exclusive spa-like environment away from the hustle of real-life everyday Bombay. Rose remembers taking a boy there once, who was darker-skinned than her, and he was asked to show his passport and turned away when he couldn't. She left with him.

Still, she had a great time and she wasn't prepared to give it up when she had to move back to the UK. So, when she arrived in London, she got herself a secretarial job in the City. She says it wasn't hard to do – after all, she had excellent qualifications and had already worked in a prestigious secretarial position back in India. I suspect, at the time, it wasn't easy. Rose must have had to do some impressive hustling.

She was single-minded. She knew what she wanted. While Clara had become a nurse and Nan had dreamed of becoming a teacher, Rose knew that being the 'right' sort of secretary would mean she could get close to the kind of circles she wanted to be in. Rose was a very bright, beautiful young woman and she wanted to make the most of it.

Despite having to walk across the whole of London to work every day because she couldn't afford the bus, it was definitely the life of glamour, or at least glamour-adjacent, that she craved – hanging out with powerful men and wearing little white gloves and hats to work every day. She had an aristocratic boss who she would have to help prepare for weekends at Balmoral with the Queen Mother. He would give her a pheasant every Christmas, which she would cook for the whole extended family on Boxing Day.

She shared a flat in Kensington with a model; she probably could have been one herself if she'd wanted. Her outfits at that time were breathtaking – I would kill to have looked like that, while at the same time cannot possibly even imagine having to do the work that must have gone into it. She had a great figure and the 1950s look suited her perfectly. Plus, the hair-dos, the corsetry, the impeccable make-up, the uncomfortable shoes!

She didn't just look incredible. She made friends, and went to dances, and also had an interesting job at a time when that wasn't necessarily the norm for a girl like her. She was self-sufficient when she could have got away with not being, which is a great example to me – I try to think of it when I'm really sick of adulting, and want to curl up in a ball and cry for my mum instead of paying the gas bill. She went out of her way to be independent and she made the most of it.

Basically, she was truly staunch.

Present Day

While Nan and Rose are not the most mobile, they are both blessed with an intrepid spirit that never fails to impress me. Fortunately, Ann is blessed with a getting-shit-done spirit that none of the rest of us has, even though we enjoy talking about our grand plans a lot.

Ann was the only one of us to bring a guidebook, and she has made a list of all the places she would like to see, and a schedule for the best way to go about it. She sits over breakfast each day, marking pages in the guidebook and making lists. As we get to know them, our friends at the hotel get involved and make suggestions.

And so begins a routine whereby we alternate days: one day staying local and having a bit of a rest, one day going off on an adventure. A few times our excursions had to be cancelled or postponed at the last minute, due to tiredness or low-level illness, but we did really well in getting out to see the area. We would hire a driver for the day and stick Rose's wheelchair in the back in case she needed it.

During the complex negotiations with drivers, as always, I'm glad Ann is there. We walk into the village and find the taxi rank, where all the drivers hang out. Ann tells them where we want to go and I try my best not to agree enthusiastically with the first convoluted plan they come up with. I keep quiet while Ann gets her map out and organizes a detailed schedule. I'm just there to keep her company while walking into the village, really.

We'll then go and pick up Nan and Rose from the hotel. The taxis we get vary wildly when it comes to model, size, air conditioning and driver friendliness.

I'm always in the middle seat and Nan constantly elbows me in the side. I try to take deep breaths and remember that she's had double knee surgery that probably makes this much more uncomfortable for her than it is for me. Rose always sits in the front and chats with the driver, and also bears the brunt of the terror of driving on the roads in India. From the front seat, she gets to see the mopeds, cows, rickety vans and buses with people hanging out on the roof coming right at us.

As well as travelling to all of the nearby towns and cities, we pore through the guidebook for all sorts of oddities that we are excited to visit.

We all love the Menezes Braganza Pereira House in Chandor. Nobody that we asked about it at the hotel had ever heard of it, but it's strange and full of stories. My favourite sort of experience.

When we arrive, at first we can't find it. When we do, we're still not sure we're in the right place. It's a Portuguese-style house in a small village, built in the seventeenth century.

It's big but not huge, and is now divided into an east wing and a west wing. Different branches of the family took over each half.

We read that guided tours of the house are available, but they don't seem to be very well organized. We ring the doorbell and meet Mrs Braganza, who lives in the west wing and claims to be the twelfth generation to occupy the house. She asks us for a donation, and sticks it in the pocket of her dress, before padding off in her slippers and expecting us to follow behind.

It's hard to tell how old Mrs Braganza is, but if I had to guess, based on first impressions I'd say somewhere around 150–200 years old. She seems ancient, even compared to the collective age of our little group. She's wearing a lovely fitted, patterned blue dress that looks straight out of the 1950s, and I covet it deeply. She's a chic old lady, with a stern manner. Even Rose follows behind her obediently.

She shows us a lot of family photographs and seems a bit sniffy about Mrs Pereira, her distant cousin who lives next door, who she implies is from a less smart branch of the family. I love these little glimpses of family rivalry and bitchiness. They make me feel at home.

She gives us the grand tour, showing us all of her treasures along the way. Some of these are truly stunning old Venetian glass mirrors and chandeliers, but she seems just as proud of her snow globes and some old beer mats that somebody from Germany gave her. It's genuinely bizarre. We are not permitted to take photographs, and Ann gets in trouble for getting bored and wandering off.

Mrs Braganza reverently shows us the tiny private chapel, which even feels somewhat holy to a semi-heathen like me. Apparently, there's a fingernail of Saint Francis Xavier in there. We leave Nan alone for a few minutes to have a good pray.

By the time we move into the second half of the house, we're kind of over it. The east wing is pretty much the same but not as good, and Mrs Pereira is terrifying. We try to get round as quickly as possible, but she refuses to allow it and insists on showing us every little thing. She also seems fairly antagonistic towards her relative/house-mate/neighbour. This sort of thing amuses me no end, particularly in older people, where somehow the pettiness is even funnier.

By the time we've done the full rounds, we're quite glad to get out. We don't manage to escape before Mrs Pereira passes us a wooden box and instructs us to put a further donation inside. Outside, Chandor itself is lovely. It's one of my favourite little towns, with its pretty church complete with Braganza mausoleum and market stalls selling pottery.

We visit a few towns and cities of varying sizes during the course of our travels. We go to Old Goa, which once had a larger population than London and was known as 'the Rome of the East'. It still has some magnificent churches. Despite all the impressive architecture and religious relics, the thing that gets me most is a wall of Mother Teresa quotes at the Basilica of Bom Jesus do Monte, which makes me tear up with pure emotion. It says:

Love begins at home, and it is not how much we do . . .
But how much love we put in that action.
Not all of us can do great things,
But we can do small things with great love.
God has not called me to be successful . . .
He called me to be faithful.
If you judge people you have no time to love them.
Spread love everywhere you go.
Let no one ever come to you without leaving happier.
What can you do to promote world peace?
Go home and love your family.

I suspect it's the sort of thing I would usually eye with scepticism, but something about it on that day speaks to me deeply. I guess I ruin the spiritual element of it, though, because pretty much the first thing I do is – obviously – Instagram the shit out of it.

We visit a lot of churches. There's one I especially like in Panaji, which is the capital of Goa. Panaji is a nice city where I feel very at home, although we have the one over-priced and disappointing touristy lunch of our whole trip there. However, my favourite town is Margao. It's not far from us and it's just an ordinary medium-sized town. Its ordinariness is exactly what I like about it. We walk around the narrow, congested streets, which have no pavement and a hundred mopeds zooming towards you at any one time. My favourite part is a dusty junction called Times Square, which has precisely nothing in common with its namesake in New York.

There is really nothing to see there, and no particular reason to hang around. However, we go into the spice market, which is a covered market much like the bazaar in Istanbul or the medina in Marrakech, only a lot smaller and not in any way ornate or beautiful. It is in a shabby, grey-coloured building and stretches for miles.

Inside, it is cramped, crowded and boiling hot. There are dozens of stalls crammed in, basically just trestle tables with plastic awnings. The walkways in between are them so narrow you have to walk in hunched single file. It is like an ordinary fruit and veg market at home, but inside a vast labyrinth that smells strongly of delicious spices and is hotter than the actual sun. I absolutely love it.

There is nothing touristy to buy here. As well as spices there are general groceries, *ladoos* and all sorts of other sweets, and household goods. There's the odd clothes stall, but they all seem to be selling the sort of clothes you could buy on a market stall in London: polyester dresses and football shirts, a lot of cheap knickers.

I've got sweat pouring down my back and I'm getting elbowed on all sides, but I am at my happiest. I love pretending I live in a place I'm visiting and this is definitely the closest I've got here. Nan is chatting to the shopkeepers in Urdu and Rose is stocking up on all the spices she needs for her legendary curry recipe. They even rediscover some (to my taste) revolting Indian sweets that they used to eat as children and have never tasted again until today.

It's so hot and labyrinthine, we physically can't stay in there too long, which is a shame as I would otherwise happily have wandered around all day. It is admittedly a relief to get outside. By the time we get out, we all look as if we have been in a sauna.

I browse some renegade roadside stalls while the others go and sit on a bench in the little municipal gardens while we wait for our taxi driver to pick us up. I buy a little beaded bracelet from a lady and her husband. A couple of weeks later, I run into the husband when we go to the touristy Anjuna market in northern Goa. He recognizes me instantly and greets me like an old friend.

'Of course I recognize you. You bought the bracelet from my wife. You were the one white girl in Margao market!'

This so delights me, and I'm not sure if he realizes how much he has made my day.

Present Day

In the hotel and in restaurants – pretty much everywhere we go – the four of us are the only group of women here on our own. We stand out a mile (for various reasons, I suppose) and I can see that people are confused by us. They can't quite work out the relationships.

Because I am by far the youngest, with a bunch of elders and clearly no husband or children, people seem to assume I'm a lot younger than I am. They must think I am an extremely haggard teenager. They also seem to think it's OK to approach us in a way that I don't think they would if we had a man with us. I find this deeply annoying. Nan and Rose do not. They just love any excuse to have a chat.

'This must be a tremendous morale boost for you, darling!' Nan exclaims frequently, when yet another creepy dude approaches us.

I mean:

a) Feminism, and

b) I'm not *that* in need of a morale boost and I don't care for the implication that I am, thank you.

'I like your smile!' is shouted at me a lot.

You know how a lot of people have the problem of 'bitchy resting face'? I have the opposite issue. This is a problem everywhere I go, but never more so than in India. I have an overly friendly face and people often take this as licence to approach me, and then refuse to go away. There is something about me that apparently screams 'please bother me'.

The catcalling etiquette here is baffling. Bizarre things get shouted at me in the street, and men frequently make slightly threatening sort of clicky-hissy noises at me while not making eye contact. However, there is also a certain level of deference, by which men don't look at me directly and will ask my grandmother and aunts' permission to address me.

As for so many reasons, I am so glad that I have Ann with me. Through sheer force of will, she has the power of being able either to charm or freeze out whoever she wants to with a small eyebrow movement or hand gesture.

'No, thank you,' she will say politely but firmly.

No apology. No explanation. No budging.

Nobody ever questions her or bothers her further – or is remotely offended.

I wonder if this is a form of staunchness that is even learnable. I have the charm, sometimes, but it's indiscriminate. It's like in sci-fi movies when superheroes haven't learned to control their powers yet. I just can't get the balance right. Although, by this age, I'm beginning to wonder whether I'm ever going to be staunch to the fierce degree that Ann is.

I'm not sure if it's because I'm young(ish) or Western, but everywhere I go, people want to chat and take selfies with me – or 'click pics', as this is hilariously known locally. As I'm small and dark, and usually wearing a kaftan bought on a market stall, I like to think I fit right in, but disappointingly, this is not actually the case. My fringe gets a lot of comments; people don't seem to have fringes in India.

After we get back and I discuss this with other people who have been to India, I find that it is a very common practice. People here are friendly and inquisitive about foreigners. It seems to be a self-perpetuating phenomenon – one person will chat and ask for a picture, then other people will over-hear and want to get involved. Before I know what has happened, a large queue will have formed.

Apparently this is particularly common in small villages and towns; or at tourist attractions, where there are a lot of domestic tourists who might also be from smaller places.

I honestly feel like I get a small taste of what it must be like to be Madonna going out in public. It holds us up when we're out and about. The first time it happens – two women come up to me in Panaji, grinning and miming camera-clicking motions – I am so confused, I think they must be talking to somebody else. Maybe someone they know, or Britney Spears, is standing behind me.

Then they both put their arms around me, press their faces up to mine on either side, and snap about a hundred photos on their phones. Then they have a little chat with each other about the fact that I have large sunglasses on, so they reach into their handbags and get out *their* sunglasses, which they both put on for more photos. One of them has a baby in a pushchair, so they haul the baby out and hold him up so that he can also be in a photograph with me. The baby cries throughout and I don't blame him. I'm not Britney Spears. He does not want his photograph taken with me. Perhaps his mum will show him these photographs one day and try to explain to him. I expect he will be just as confused as I am.

The two women both hug me before they carry on their way, giggling happily. I am so discombobulated by what the hell just happened that I – shamefully but automatically – check they haven't nicked my purse out of my bag.

Back in Benaulim, it happens a few times on the beach, but not as often. Anywhere there are crowds, it's open season on selfie time. At the touristy churches in Old Goa, or in the streets and markets further afield, there is often a long queue for having photographs taken with me.

The irony is I am horribly unphotogenic, and these strangers must now have camera rolls full of crap pictures of a sweaty, lank-fringed woman at various Indian tourist landmarks. It's very harmless and it's quite funny.

It even happens to Nan and Rose, at length, on our day trip to the Aguada Fort. The fort is (logically) at the top of a hill, overlooking the water, and there is no such thing as the dreaded 'health and safety' here. There's no 'it's political correctness gone mad!', much is the pity. To explore the fort, you walk along the slippery, chalky track up the hill, in order to then walk around the edge of some very high-up crumbling walls, where there is no safety rail or anything to stop you falling off the steep cliff edge.

Ann and I want to go and have a quick look, so we leave Nan and Rose sitting on a bench at the bottom, while we join the crowds to go up and walk around. As usual, the joke is on me. While I am perfectly capable of dashing up there with both fitness and enthusiasm, Rose and Nan watching serenely from below, I am also extremely clumsy. Almost immediately, I slip over on the dusty ground and scrape my foot. A big flap of skin is hanging off, but I don't say anything as there'll only be a fuss. Once we get up there, I'm not scared of heights, but it does feel a bit perilous to be skirting these high walls, single file as that's all there is room for, right on the edge of a drop down to the sea. All the young Indian tourists around are casually laughing, chatting and attempting to take selfies with me, while I grimace and try my best to cling to the disconcertingly smooth, shiny fort walls.

'If anyone was ever going to have a comedy accident in a place like this,' I say to Ann, 'you know it would be me.'

'Don't you dare, girl,' she replies. 'What would I tell your grandmother?'

Like my sister, Ann is very practical. As such, she despairs of me at times. My sister is – entirely justifiably and with fondness – forever rolling her eyes and saying 'oh my God, I thought you were supposed to be clever' when I do something illogical and stupid. I can sense the same feeling in Ann.

Fortunately, I manage to make it off the walls and back

down the hill otherwise unscathed. We get back to the bench where we left the others to find a crowd swarming around them as if they are a particularly interesting part of the tourist attraction.

We learn that the crowd is made up of an entire extended family, two brothers and their wives and their many, many children of various ages. The youngest is a tiny baby. They have propped the baby up on Rose's lap while the adults all snap hundreds of photographs.

'I'm not sure what's going on,' Rose says, 'but they seem very pleased about it.'

Of course, when they see us, we must be in the photographs as well. Ann, of course, politely declines and they are neither offended by this nor keen to challenge it, such is the Ann power. I have to pose with the wives, who are both much prettier than I am. My nan tells them in Urdu how beautiful they are.

So, of course, next they are enchanted that Nan can speak Urdu and have to take a dozen photographs of her. By the end of it, I feel pretty much like a hungry exploited model must do at the end of the working day.

But the selfie thing is generally so bizarre, it's kind of fun. It's only when the dudes are really intense about it that things can get a bit unsettling.

One evening we get a car and drive out of town to a restaurant called Martin's Corner, which is legendary and very popular with locals and tourists. There is live music and you can get a lobster dinner for a price that is ridiculously low by Western standards.

We drink fenny cocktails and eat whole lobsters. There is a guy playing a Casio keyboard and doing covers of light pop hits from around 1960–1985. This is the style of live music in most of the restaurants here and we love it, some of us in a more ironic way than others. My favourites are the inevitable Lionel Richie covers. One night on Benaulim beach, 'Careless Whisper' is an unexpected and ridiculously exciting bonus. I video it on my phone and send it to my sister. Sometimes we still watch it.

We drink some more cocktails and sing along to Abba and the Carpenters. It's really fun here. It's a Saturday night and lots of extended families around us are having dinner out. We are, as always, the only table of women.

The waiter, whose name badge says he is called Frank, keeps stopping by the table to see if everything is OK, looking at everyone apart from me. Even without eye contact, the service is impressively attentive.

'And, may I ask a favour . . .' he says eventually. 'I would like permission to take a picture with the young lady.'

He looks at the others expectantly. Ann shrugs: I'm big enough to speak up for myself. Nan and Rose both immediately express delight at this and agree loudly and enthusiastically on my behalf.

'He likes you, Ells!' they exclaim, as if a fifty-year-old stranger called Frank is totally my type and exactly what I've been waiting for all these years.

When I say I find the whole thing a little bit odd, they scoff.

'He's sweet. Just play along. You'll make his day.'

I think they enjoy the collective attention on our group.

Frank keeps hovering around the table, checking if we need more drinks while our glasses are still full, and reminding us repeatedly that we mustn't leave before he gets his picture.

When we have finished our dinner, he gets me to stand with him very formally on a small flight of stairs. He puts his arm around me stiffly, he immaculate in his starched, short-sleeved white shirt. Me sweating in my baggy Batman T-shirt and a long Seventies skirt I bought second-hand when I was twenty. I have no idea why he wants to have his picture taken with me.

He takes this extremely seriously and is determined to get the correct pose, giving terse instructions and rejecting several shots. I genuinely start to wonder if we've misunderstood his request and he thinks this is our official engagement photograph. It's only when our taxi arrives to take us back to the hotel that he relents and is forced to accept one of the inferior shots. Otherwise, I think we might have been there for hours. I wonder what he'll do with the pictures and can only conclude it's like people who take videos at gigs and then never watch them again. It's about the getting, not the having. I guess I can relate.

However, Frank is bettered a few nights later by Dev. Dev's restaurant is on my daily round of stalls, right at the end of a small strip of shops before the dirt track down to the beach. It's the emptiest of all the restaurants, and the décor is – let's say – incongruous. Dev is a slightly chubby guy in a tight shirt and he evidently wants us to think he is very cool. He tells us he has friends in Manchester and he has aspirations to be an international DJ. He seems like a bit of a local big shot.

I think his restaurant would be a lot more appealing if it were decorated more casually, like all the other beach shacks. However, Dev has decked his place out like an Ibiza super-club, as imagined by someone who has never been to Ibiza. The chairs are upholstered in brightly coloured crushed velvet and the lights are rigged up so that they flash in different colours. We feel kind of bad for him, so eventually we agree to go to his restaurant.

Fortunately, we are not quite the only people there, but it's still pretty awkward. It's a vast restaurant, and there's just us and a Russian family on the other side of the room. Dev rhapsodises about his cocktail menu and says he teaches bartending courses in Mumbai, then does not have the ingredients available to make Ann a Martini. We're not sure what's in Rose's Piña Colada, but it's definitely not quite right. The ladies are understandably getting irritated, and I just want to fall through a hole in the floor and disappear. Poor old Dev's tight shirt is getting sweatier by the minute.

'With the greatest respect, may I ask you a question?' Obviously, he addresses the elders of the table and I brace myself for the inevitable selfie. 'I would like to present a gift to the young lady. Simply as a friend.'

This is so leftfield we are all genuinely dumbstruck. Which is how I, who always insist on paying my own way on a date lest I be beholden to a man, end up sitting very awkwardly at the table and being made to close my eyes while he puts a clunky plastic necklace and bracelet on me. There's then an ensuing palaver when he insists on accompanying me to the mirror hanging outside the loos, so we can both admire this great and not-at-all-inappropriate gift. Dev keeps nodding and smiling at me, and I do my best to fashion my face into an expression that is both polite and not too encouraging.

I find myself wondering for the rest of the trip quite how this transpired: has he been waiting for this occasion and prepared in advance, or does Dev have a box of plastic jewellery stashed under the bar, just in case a woman he likes the look of happens to come in for dinner? I remain mystified by the whole thing.

Still, the weight of these gifts weighs heavily upon me for the course of our dinner. The four of us spend the rest of the evening looking at each other sideways and trying not to laugh.

'Any girlfriends with birthdays coming up?' Ann asks me with a wink.

Actually, it's not a bad idea.

The whole exchange is just so awful and uncomfortable. I'm sure it is well intentioned on his part, but I'm just not sure what I'm supposed to do. I have no idea what the correct response to this is, or how I am supposed to behave.

I guess maybe it is just a nice gift to give a 'friend' but, having been quite natural and relaxed before, I'm now too nervous even to smile at Dev, in case he takes it the wrong way. But then I feel guilty, like perhaps I'm being unfriendly. In turn, I then begin to feel cross that the onus is on me.

When we leave, even Nan and my aunts are a bit befuddled by the whole situation.

'My goodness, for once I didn't really know what to say!' Rose exclaims. 'How awkward.'

I feel guilty that, whatever his intention, Dev's gift has the opposite of the desired effect. We do not go back to his restaurant again. Every time I walk past, I wave sheepishly before scuttling off as quickly as possible.

Present Day

The older I get, the more I make a point in life to try to avoid either giving or receiving advice. It's very rarely a good idea. Resentment always happens one way or the other.

My friends are so different from me. Our decision-making processes – and what we want to achieve from them – are not in any way the same. I know myself quite well by now. However, many of my friends seem to have a lot of opinions about my life. So many well intentioned but utterly unhelpful opinions.

By this point, I have some close friends I have known for a few years now, who only know me as single and chaotic. They have no memory of 'Ellie and K'. They never came round for dinner in our old flat, or realize that for over a decade I had no juicy gossip in my life, ever. This is still mind-blowing to me, it's so bizarre. It's like they only half know me, and I keep having to remind them that my life used to be very different.

They don't even realize that, three years on, I still wake

up some mornings confused that K isn't there. We were so close for so long, it still feels like a phantom limb and I'm semi-resigned to the fact that maybe it always will.

It also means that I have girlfriends who have been with their boyfriends for two or three years, and think that – compared to me, the depressed spinster borderline-alcoholic with the hilarious self-deprecating stories – they have all the answers and can advise me on relationships. I nod and smile politely, and say I'm happy for them that they have found something that works so well for them. They never pick up on the subtext of this, which is *good for you, not for me*.

There are also the friends who helpfully say they remember *exactly* what it was like being single and worried about life (when they were fucking twenty-six, or whatever), or that they envy me living alone because they're *so* independent that they actually really enjoy it when their husband goes away for, like, four days for work.

Crucially, I manage not to snap at them that I have lived with two men quite harmoniously – to varying degrees – and I have a pretty good idea of what it's all about, even if that's not what I'm doing at the moment. I do not point out that the relationships they're humblebragging about all over the place ('relationships are *hard*!', 'you have to compromise sometimes!') are not even a quarter as long as my most significant relationship.

Even more importantly, I do not point out that I think their husbands and boyfriends are not necessarily worth boasting about quite so loudly. I have these thoughts, because

I am a horrible and judgemental person, but I manage not to say them out loud. However, the truth is, I just can't seem to rouse any interest in nice, ordinary men.

The problem is, I just cannot settle. Like my great-grandmother before me, I am incapable of settling. Occasionally, I think maybe I should try to live more like some of these friends – like, maybe it would be kind of nice just to have a decent, medium-funny boyfriend with a beard and a Gap jumper to watch boxsets and eat a baked potato with or whatever. But every time I attempt to consider it, the rogue voice in my head starts shouting loudly. Fuck that, I want to marry Picasso! Fuck that, I want to marry David Bowie and Ted Hughes and George Harrison. I still can't quite give up on the idea of extraordinary.

'What exactly do you *want*?' Ann asks me, sitting on our balcony overlooking the sea, with a glass of wine from the minibar.

'Ted Hughes, basically,' I say, without really thinking about it.

'A man who drove two women to suicide. Great plan, Ells.' She laughs, even though we both know it's not actually that funny.

I may not be prepared to take advice from my friends, but I come to realize pretty quickly that Ann is a good person to take advice from. While we're away, she and I talk about boys a lot. We talk about everything a lot, actually. It's the most time I've ever spent with her, by a long way, and getting to know my glamorous youngest great-aunt better is one of the huge joys of the trip for me.

If you don't know her well, she can seem intimidating. She's good-looking, witty and clever. Cleverness somehow seems to come out of her pores; you could know it without ever even speaking to her. She's a retired teacher and she has the greatest breadth of knowledge and interests of anyone I know: she genuinely loves books, art and theatre, but also politics and sport. She's seen every film and read every book, and doesn't show off about it – but if you happen to mention it, she's a real enthusiast. She loves reading the Classics and watching live athletics and keeping up with any and all world events, to name but a few hobbies. I know very few people who have the combination of academic intelligence and common sense that Ann does.

She decided to come on the trip at the last minute. She lived in Germany and Hong Kong, and now divides her time between the UK, Australia and Cyprus. But she had not set foot in India since she left at the age of two. She had no memory of living there.

She is one of the few people in my family never to have been divorced. She met her husband when they were still at school. They travelled the world and had a fabulous life together. Then when he became unexpectedly ill, she spent many years looking after him, until he died a few years ago.

She's only in her early seventies and I cannot stress enough that she is a very hot woman. She could definitely get herself another dude if she wanted to. But she adamantly doesn't want to. She does not want to look after another man. I can understand this.

She has incredible friends, goes to every art exhibition in

London and sees every film, and travels a great deal. She makes it look fabulous. I would happily emulate her life when I am in my seventies. In fact, our lives are not that dissimilar now, only she has more time for fun than I do. I only wonder if I would be sad to miss out on the bit in between, with the husband and the children. She now has grandchildren who bring her a lot of joy. It would be a shame not to have that.

While we're away, I tell her more and more about the ongoing saga with The Lecturer. She is appalled.

'No, Ells! Do not put your eggs in that basket. Do not put one single, solitary egg in that basket.'

The thing is, whenever I tell anyone about our relationship, it sounds a bit lame. I don't even know how to refer to it – I'm certainly not permitted to call him my boyfriend, but saying we're 'just friends' doesn't sound quite correct either.

I argue the case for him anyway. I'm not even sure why. I can barely even justify our relationship to myself. Even my therapist says she has no idea what exactly I get out of it.

Still, I tell Ann that he's supposed to be coming to stay for the weekend when we get back, and I'm hoping we can 'discuss our relationship'.

'Oh, for goodness' sake. Why do you need to *discuss your relationship*? That's not a good sign. You shouldn't have to discuss it. That all sounds like very hard work.'

Again, I know she is right. This really strikes a chord with me, despite what I've been trying to tell myself – all my 'proper' relationships, where we've both really been in it together, have not been this much hard work.

Ann's advice means a lot to me because, I discover, we are very similar in many ways. We are a great tag-team on the trip, making sure that we each have some alone time, which is necessary for both of us – I go swimming in the sea, she lies by the pool and reads. Then we drink beers together and hang out on the balcony, chatting.

We have similar interests and temperaments, but as the trip goes on, I realize she is a lot braver and a lot more straightforward than I am. Maybe it's a part of staunchness that comes with age – maybe you get tired of the bullshit and of making things more palatable for other people. I hope so, as I would like to be more like her, in this respect and many others.

I've been working in therapy at trying to speak my mind more, worry less about what other people think, over-coming my outsized fear of conflict. Sometimes now in these situations I try to think of Ann. She has become one of my barometers.

She has no time for small talk, one of the other ways that she can seem intimidating. But, more satisfyingly, you can go right into the big subjects with her and she doesn't turn a hair. She and I take to going for long walks together, just the two of us, on the long roads into the nearby towns, that are full of tuk-tuks, mopeds and cows. It's about the walking rather than the destination. We walk as far as we can go along the road, stop in town for a lime soda, then walk back again, talking continuously.

'Did you ever experience any sexism in the workplace? Do you think your daughter will marry her girlfriend? Do you mind both of your children living in Australia? Did you know you would marry your husband when you were teenagers at school together?'

She is also the family truth-teller. I have a weird compulsion to make every bad thing that has ever happened to me into a funny story. I definitely get this tendency from my grandmother, who has passed it down to all of us. Ann has no time for such rose-tinted spectacles and for that I have the greatest respect for her.

It's through her that I get to the bottom of a lot of the family myths. When Nan tells a story, it's invariably the sunny side. She's told them like this so many times she believes it: everything was lovely, it all worked out fine in the end.

'It didn't happen quite like that, Dot,' Ann will say gently.

She will tell the real story, factually and calmly, and everyone will remember that, yes, that is how it actually happened. It doesn't cause a row; nothing bad happens.

I vow to stop putting a spin on things, which sometimes I do without even really knowing why. It certainly doesn't do any good. I not only want to be more staunch, but to give my time and energy only to the things that actually matter – in short, I want to try to be a bit more like Ann.

October 1948

A few months after Rose moved down to London by herself, the family followed behind her, as soon as they could. Initially, they moved into rented rooms in Chiswick along with Dolly's sister and her family. Then they received a British Legion grant being offered to re-settlers to help them buy a house: £250 to act as a deposit.

Dolly and Chum bought their house in Acton, West London, for £2,000. That obviously seems ridiculous compared to London house prices today, but Nan reminds me that this was a huge amount of money to them at the time. I remember that house as being enormous – as children, my cousin Nic and I would use the three storeys' worth of staircase as the perfect backdrop for us to perform choreographed renditions of 'It's a Hard Knock Life' – but when I see pictures of it now, it looks small compared to my memories. It was a very nice, ordinary terraced house in a nice quiet street off the main high street.

Ann and Sam, the two youngest children of the second

marriage, have lives very different from their older siblings. They grew up in a completely different culture on the other side of the world.

The older children were brought up as the little prince and princesses of the Raj. Their childhood was full of servants and afternoon teas being served on the lawn. Ann was two when they left India, and Sam was the only child to be born in the UK, unlike their older siblings. So Ann and Sam had a typical upbringing in 1950s West London. Their house was opposite the park, where they would go to the fair when it came to town; they went to the ordinary local school and went into town on a Saturday, and occasionally got a bus into the West End. They certainly didn't have servants.

Despite having English surnames and RP accents, we were essentially an immigrant family. Not only was the UK totally foreign, and this whole new life took a lot of acclimatising to, but the Indian customs of the family remained. There was curry for lunch every Sunday and Dolly would go on shopping expeditions to Southall to get the exact right type of Brinjal pickle, which you just can't get in an English supermarket.

To this day, the family slang is still sprinkled with the odd Anglo-Indian word or phrase. When I was little, I always assumed everyone understood what they meant. Nan would ask me if I wanted *unda bunda* (egg) for breakfast, and tell me to *juldi* (hurry up) and get in the *gussel* (bath). She would sing me Indian lullabies that she remembered from her ayah, that I still know word for word. In fact, it's only on our trip to India that I learn what some of it actually means.

When I think about it now, the staunch resilience – particularly of Dolly and Chum – makes me feel somewhat ashamed of my own inability to get my shit together. They had to take jobs where they could, and they worked hard and without complaint.

Some elements of living in London must still have been baffling. Someone smashed the pot plants that they put outside in the front garden for no good reason. They were robbed when a man knocked at the door, asking for directions – Chum asked him in and got out his *A–Z* – while an accomplice broke in at the back and grabbed Dolly's handbag and everything else they could get their hands on. Still, the family became a part of the community. They made great friends with the Indian family who lived next door, as well as all their English neighbours. Nan's brother Bill got together with Polly, the girl who lived across the road.

Chum found a job working in the office of Smith's clock factory. Nan says he hated his job – although you'd never have known it – but his great joy was playing for the factory hockey team and occasionally going out after work to play darts.

Even Dolly, who had never cooked a meal until the age of forty-two, helped to make ends meet by working as a tea lady. She'd go out every morning at ten o'clock to take tea and biscuits around a local office, where a neighbour had got her the job.

In a practical sense, life was pretty tough, but Nan – and I don't think it's just her rose-tinted spectacles talking – remembers this as the happiest of times. They were all so grateful to be alive, to be together and to have a roof over their heads.

'Honestly, I can never remember any of us feeling unhappy in that house. I think it was because we used to do so much as a family. We'd play cards in the evenings, play big games of Crown and Anchor. Of course, there was no television. We just entertained ourselves as a family. We all just got on. We made the best of it and it was honestly a very happy time.'

I vow to try to remember this more.

Present Day

Anjuna Market is in northern Goa. It's a legendary tourist spot and hippie mecca, founded by hippie Western tourists in the Sixties and, according to Lonely Planet, it's 'as much part of the Goan experience as a day on the beach'.

Of all the Goa hotspots, this is the one that has been recommended me the most, by a few friends and my cool youngest cousin, Carrie. Carrie knows me very well and we have similar taste in things – so when she texts me saying I will LOVE it and absolutely must go, I really, really want to.

Going to a vast market with Nan and Rose, who can't walk too far, doesn't necessarily sound like the best idea, and Ann despises shopping (it bores the shit out of her). However, they are all invariably up for an adventure – whatever it looks like – so we decide that, if I really want to go, then all four of us are going together.

'We can always find somewhere to sit and have a drink while you look around, Ells,' is always Nan's pragmatic, and quite generous, plan.

The market is held every Wednesday and I can't wait. However, I have to. The first time we attempt to go on a Wednesday, Rose has an upset stomach and Nan is tired out, so we spend the day at the hotel instead and vow to go the next Wednesday. This sort of slowing down and going with the flow is one of the lessons this trip is teaching me. If it were just me, I always want to do all of the things all of the time. I cannot do enough things and I cannot do them quickly enough. I am beginning to realize that the world does not end if I am not constantly occupied. In fact, becoming comfortable with a more sedate pace is a great gift.

Everyone we speak to suggests going to Anjuna as early in the morning as possible, as it gets very hot and crowded as the day goes on. Of course, this in itself is quite the mission, considering how long it takes us to get ready and have breakfast every day.

Of course, on the designated day, I come back from my early morning yoga class to find the usual getting-ready chaos going on. Rose is still in the shower and Nan is debating which of her half a dozen pairs of identical white Capri pants to wear. Ann is sensibly on the balcony, reading her book and drinking tea, staying well out of the fray, like some sort of Yoda-like figure.

By the time we finish breakfast and are finally ready to go, it's nearly eleven o'clock. Anjuna is a good couple of hours' drive away, traffic and cows in the road permitting. We finally get a driver organized and bundle into the car.

As we head north of Panaji, the vibe changes. North Goa looks more like somewhere I might come on holiday if I were with my most-fun girlfriends. Driving through the beach towns of North Goa, there are posters everywhere for beach parties and live bands, signs advertising cheap massages, many fairy lights and bearded Western hippies in sarongs. In short, it's my kind of place.

They are all heading down the dirt track in the same direction, like stoned lemmings. Market stalls start to spring up as the track gets rougher. This is Anjuna Market. It's exactly like arriving at Glastonbury.

By the time we get there, the sun is beating down fiercely and the market is packed full of people. Our driver drops us off in a makeshift car park on the edges, along one side of which is a long row of mopeds and cows. We follow the flow of hippies – Rose with her walking stick, Nan holding onto my arm – and head into the market.

The first person to approach us is a sketchy-looking old man with a beard. Before we know what is happening or have the chance to stop him, he is sticking a long, sharp needle-like implement into Rose's ear and pulling out reams and reams of earwax, which he wipes off onto the heel of his own hand before going in and digging again.

'Look! Look how much!' he keeps exclaiming, pulling more and more frankly ludicrous amounts of wax out of Rose's ear and showing it to us in his hand.

It's hypnotic. It's like magic. I am amazed that much detritus could be in there. No wonder her hearing is so poor, which is a problem that she finds deeply annoying. However, despite her poor hearing and walking stick, I don't think the earwax man counted on Rose having quite so many wits about her. She is, in fact – unlike me – the last person he should have picked to try to pull off a typical tourist scam like this.

'Hang on just a minute,' Rose says loudly, while I'm still transfixed by this spectacle. 'I've got my hearing aids in. All that muck can't possibly have come out of my ear. You couldn't get *that thing* in there if you tried.'

The earwax man initially starts to argue and demand money, but Rose has a loud voice and the staunch air of unfuckable-with-ness that only comes with age. A small crowd has gathered, and their initial enthusiasm has turned to chuntering. The earwax man makes a run for it.

I think to myself that he should probably just have asked me for money and I'd have given it to him. He didn't really need to have gone to all the bother of the elaborate earwax pantomime. However, I just keep quiet.

The stalls here are much the same as everywhere else. Lots of jewellery, kaftans, big tasselled throws and various knick-knacks. Rose and I are the two of the group who enjoy buying a surplus of Indian souvenirs the most. Ann is not the least bit interested and Nan just likes the attention of getting involved and looking at things, then I get embarrassed when she fails to actually want to buy anything, so Rose and I have to buy even more to compensate for her. I feel guilty and beholden every time.

'It's their job, darling,' Nan shrugs, with the attitude she sees as only sensible. 'They'd be there on their stalls whether I'm there looking at things or not. I'm not obliged to buy anything.'

I guess she's right, but I can't shake the feeling of guilt that follows me everywhere I go. I feel like, when people are so keen for you to spend money on their stall, I should be careful not to get their hopes up. As so often in life, probably people care about what I'm doing a lot less than I assume they do.

I trail around with Rose, helping her pick out endless presents for her son, daughter-in-law and grandchildren, while my nan and Ann get increasingly bored. They eventually suggest finding somewhere to sit down and get a drink, while I go off and explore on my own.

For the first time on this holiday, I unexpectedly feel like I've been set free. I've been in the slow bubble of an alternate universe, away from everything, and it's been perfect. But here, unexpectedly, I am reminded of being back in my own life – and I realize it's actually a pretty good feeling.

I feel utterly at home here and I find myself wondering what it would be like to be here with my friends, to have a totally different sort of trip. I wonder what it would be like to be here with The Lecturer and I'm not sure. I can't imagine him in India, with his pale skin and his old cricket jumpers, but then he can be very unexpected sometimes. I send him a picture of the chaos here – the hot, dusty mixture of hippies, mopeds and cows – and wait for his pithy response. We both like to play up to our respective stereotypes. Then I put my phone away and go exploring.

So, just for an hour, I go off and I have the sort of holiday that I would have if I were here alone. I am in my element. Everyone is so friendly and it's lovely to wander around in the hot sunshine, chatting to the stallholders and hippies. I buy a bumper pack of cut-price incense, which I am constantly burning at home. I buy a little brass owl for The Lecturer, in reference to a silly long-ago joke that he has probably forgotten but still makes me laugh. I'm not sure I will even give it to him, but I buy it just in case.

I buy a couple of unbelievably cheap and lovely Indian summer dresses. I know I won't be able to wear them again for months at home, but I reason this will give me something extra to look forward to when I'm back in the midst of a grey British winter. Maybe I'll wear them around the house to cheer myself up.

I buy a ring from a lady who tells me this is her first sale of the day and will bring us both good luck. She seems so delighted about it, I choose to believe her. I wear it so often when I get home, eventually I just get a tattoo of it. I like to think it's perpetual good luck.

In an incredible coup, I find a stall selling crystals. Amid all the other hippie tat I've been buying all over the place, these are the first I've seen in India. At home, I have them dotted around my house, usually small purchases I have made because I have been having a bad day and automatically head to the local new-age shop to try and buy myself a little bit of good fortune. As if it's that easy.

The young guy running the crystal stall is wearing a tie-dye T-shirt and an air of extreme enthusiasm. On learning that I am British, he asks me if I've ever been to Glastonbury, to which I reply, 'of course, every year!'.

This used to be true. I don't mention that I haven't actually been for nearly ten years. After a couple of rainy miserable ones in a row, I decided in my late twenties that I was too old for that sort of shit any more.

He doesn't actually seem to know very much about crystals, but he offers to look up anything I want to know in a large book he has on the subject, and that's fine by me. Mostly he just wants to chat about music.

As we do so, he tactfully looks the other way as I spot a whole shelf full of crystal dildos, much like the one I have at home. Most things to do with Bad Boyfriend I have got rid of. I threw the necklace he gave me into the sea. I never even tried to get my own belongings back. It wasn't worth the hassle. It's still annoying, though. However, I still had the rose quartz dildo in the back of a drawer in my bedroom. Of course, I couldn't bring myself to use it – crystals soak up bad vibes and this one had some definite bad karma. It was the only other remaining witness to things I wish I could forget.

However, I had absolutely no idea what I could possibly do with it. It seemed wrong just to throw it away. It's not the sort of thing I can pass on or re-gift to a friend. I can't even symbolically throw it in the sea – what if it washes up on the beach and a child finds it? Apparently you are supposed to bury unwanted crystals in the ground, but I've only got pots in my garden and next door's cats are always digging things up. The whole situation could get highly embarrassing. I can't exactly take it and bury it in the local park, can I?

Suddenly it occurs to me in a flash of clarity. If I can't get rid of it, surely the next best thing is to get another one to cancel it out. Logic is not my strong point but to me this makes perfect sense and I know it is finally the solution I've been looking for. It's an instant and great relief.

I find the perfect one. It's bright yellow and interestingly patterned, which seems apt. We look it up in the book and it's made of septarian, also known as 'dragonstone'. Pleasingly, it's known as a stone for psychic protection.

It's approximately twice the size of the old rose quartz one. This seems like a good fresh start in itself – the very fact that I am able to buy it without considering the fear of anybody putting it into an unexpected orifice with no prior warning. Despite its large size, it costs the equivalent of about a tenner. The old smaller one cost about forty quid, contributing slightly to my reluctance to throw it away.

I decide, joyously, that I'll take it.

'Do you . . . ? Um,' the guy mutters awkwardly, his fluent Glastonbury chat seemingly dried up. 'You know what this is for?'

The shape is kind of a giveaway. I can't help but burst out laughing. I cheerily assure him that I do, and tuck it away in my handbag.

As I'm walking back the way I came, an old lady suddenly grabs my arm. I seem to have old lady attracting vibes, they find me everywhere I go. I turn to see that she makes my nan and aunts look like spring chickens. She grins at me toothlessly and brandishes a large basket. She looks like Mother Teresa, but older and a bit more wizened.

She takes my hand and pulls me to face her. We lock eyes. I feel a wave of pure love and joy. I'm on a high and I'm not exactly sure why. Maybe it's muscle memory of being on hallucinogenics at Glastonbury, although that was often not much fun. I once lost all of my friends and my tent after ingesting too many mushrooms and became convinced my brain was never going to go back to normal. I woke up in a puddle about twelve hours later and somebody had stolen all my cigarettes.

'You are special,' she tells me. 'I would like to give you a blessing. For good luck.'

She puts her thumb into a pot of bright red powder and presses it to my forehead. I have pretty much never been so delighted in my whole life. Maybe she gives them out to everyone, regardless of their 'special' vibes. I choose to believe not. I feel like she is genuinely transmitting some sort of magical power into my third eye. The pressure of her thumb is warm and comforting, and she leaves it there for a while. Sealing the magic in, I like to think.

She hugs me and gives me a yellow flower from her basket. It is tiny and starting to turn slightly brown. I accept it gratefully and tuck it into my plait. I then – of course – give her all of my remaining money. I'm not really sure what else one is supposed to do. When she hugs me goodbye, it feels like a fair exchange.

The high from this encounter lasts quite some time. I try to preserve my bindi for as long as I can, keeping my face out of the shower and being careful when I swim in the sea, like some kind of old-fashioned lady, doggy-paddling with my head held up out of the water. After a few days, traces of blessing still remain in my frown line. I like to think a few particles are still in there somewhere. It even takes a couple of days for the flower to drop off, even though it's entirely brown and crispy by the time it does. I think it eventually came off in the sea, which seems fitting.

I am still grinning my face off when I reluctantly walk back to find the others. I could very happily spend at least a month here, quite possibly move in. These are the sorts of places I dreamed of from about the age of eleven, when I heard Nirvana for the first time, and became obsessed with the idea of 'being cool'. I have never grown out of it. As an adult I still regularly have moments when I am filled with joy for what my tweenage self would think if she could see me now. It's generally when I get a new tattoo, or go to a gig on a weeknight.

I find the ladies where they have set up camp, outside a sort of café stall with chairs. It really is exactly like being at Glastonbury, if that helps you to picture it – picnic chairs under a tarpaulin in the sunshine, with Indian dance music playing. They look utterly out of place but it is a familiar scene to me.

Except that there is a cow grazing right next to them, and a table where a group of women are shelling some sort of nuts. I sit down and order a beer. Ann takes one look at my new bindi and bursts out laughing.

'Typical Ells! What an earth have you been up to? Knowing you, I bet you paid about twenty quid for that!'

I keep quiet about the crystal dildo in my handbag.

They all laugh even more when I sit and take a whole series of selfies, to demonstrate me simultaneously drinking a beer and sporting a bindi. The juxtaposition amuses me.

What also amuses me is the lavatory at this market bar. Every time I go to the loo here, I weirdly kind of hope for a weird or gross Indian toilet, so that I can feel like I'm having an authentic experience. I mean, I was warned about them, but disappointingly at most of the places we have been, they have been pretty ordinary. This one is a smelly hole in the ground behind a rickety sort of bamboo cubicle – pleasingly, it is definitely the worst one yet and I am delighted.

After two beers, we decide we should probably find our driver and get out of here. Walking back towards the car park, taking my time and lagging behind the others, I spot possibly the most beautiful man I have seen since we arrived in India. I don't even really need to describe him by this point, do I? Long-haired, bearded, skinny, suntanned, tattooed and shirtless – check. Oh and of course – *of course* – he has a battered old acoustic guitar slung over one shoulder.

Our eyes meet and we smile at each other. I keep walking. I can't shake the feeling I am being watched. When I turn around, he is following me. I smile at him and look away, and keep walking. This happens several times and I must admit I am quite enjoying it. I'm quite good at flirting until I have to talk, when I invariably become clumsy and awkward.

'Hello, beautiful.' The boy comes up behind me and taps me on the shoulder.

'Oh . . . Um. Hi.'

I wasn't expecting to actually have to talk. Close up, the boy is even more beautiful than I first thought and definitely a lot younger than me.

'What's your name?'

'Eleanor.'

'Nice. I'm Mohammed. I just arrived here, slept on the beach last night. This place is cool, right?'

He grins at me. He speaks good English, with a slightly surfy American accent, like he learned his vocabulary from watching early Keanu Reeves films or similar. Actually, scratch that, he'd be far too young. It's probably, like, *High School Musical* or something else I am too old to understand. I bet this kid doesn't know who Bill and Ted are, let alone has seen *My Own Private Idaho*.

'So, beautiful, shall we go for a walk together? We could go to the beach, have a drink, whatever . . .'

'Ha! I'm sorry, I can't.'

'Would you like to come to the beach party with me tonight?'

'I'm sorry, I can't. I have to go.'

'Well, can I at least have your number?'

'I would like to say yes . . . But you see, I'm here with my grandmother. So . . . I can't.'

He, understandably, looks very confused.

'So can I have your number or what?'

'Sorry, no. There just isn't any point.'

For a second, all I want is to run off with him. Maybe just for a few days, maybe forever. He is legitimately beautiful.

He seems fun. He is young and carefree. In short, the ideal holiday romance. Before we got here, I was spending so much time worrying about the future, about all the things I don't have. Maybe, if circumstances were different, a no-strings holiday fling would be the ideal thing. The idea of distraction and ego boost combined suddenly seems quite appealing.

Did I mention he was fucking beautiful? The kind of guy who wouldn't look twice at me at home. I'm not being self-deprecating, it's true. All the gorgeous leggy art students in Brighton and the trendier parts of East London would have gone crazy over this boy, for sure. Just for a second, I actually want to cry that I can't go with him.

'I have to go.'

I skip off to catch up with the others, who are getting into the car. Mohammed follows me at a casual distance and is still watching us as we drive off. He waves at me as I watch him recede in the mirror. I smile, and wave back until he goes out of sight.

November 1948

When Nan was still in Scotland, she happened to run into her friend Penny on Paisley High Street. She knew Penny from back in India, and their families were now in similar positions. The two of them stayed in touch, and when Penny got a place at Ashford Hospital in Middlesex to train as a nurse, she suggested that Nan apply and come along with her.

Nan had never had any interest whatsoever in becoming a nurse. However, she didn't have anything better to do or many other options. So, she applied and got a place on the course, mostly just so she could hang out with her fun pal Penny.

Unlike her older sister, my Auntie Clara, Nan turned out not to have much aptitude for nursing, although she loved the camaraderie of it.

'There was so much laughter, and *fun*. The fun we had. I loved it. I made great friends.'

Clara had already qualified as a nurse, and was a brilliant one. She also applied to Ashford Hospital and got a job there as Ward Sister. She ended up spending much of her time covering for her own naughty little sister, who was not particularly interested in becoming a brilliant nurse.

When asked of her memories of Ashford Hospital, the first thing that springs to Nan's mind now is that there was a pub across the road called the Stag and Hounds. She spent a lot of time chatting to boys there, along with Penny and their other roommate Doris, who was from Jamaica. The three of them had a great time.

Nan remembers once, over Ascot weekend, a group of boys in an open-top car pulling up in the street outside and asking Nan and Penny if they wanted to come along to Ascot races with them.

'All right,' they said, and climbed in.

They had a lovely day at Ascot – Nan still remembers speeding through the countryside and feeling wonderfully glamorous. However, they were supposed to be on duty at the hospital that evening; they got back horribly late and were in big trouble with Auntie Clara.

They went out to dances at Hammersmith Palais a lot. Nan is still a champion at the jitterbug. Her nursing course was supposed to be three years long, but she never finished it.

One weekend her cousin Josephine asked if she wanted to go with her to Heathrow Airport, where she was meeting a friend who worked there as an aircraft engineer. His name was Jack and he was another ex-British Raj pal, who had worked in aviation back in Karachi but had now also resettled in West London.

Nan suspected that Josephine had a bit of a crush on Jack,

but all hopes of that were blown right out of the water the minute he and Nan laid eyes on each other. While she says she's not sure she believes in love at first sight, 'we absolutely fancied each other'.

He looked like Clark Gable, with brown eyes and a twirly moustache. Nan also says he was very easy-going with a generous nature, and loads of fun to be around. Which, for a time, presumably made up for the fact that he was also a helpless gambler and a bit of a player.

Nan didn't have particularly high hopes of being able to keep him under control, but she fell head over heels in love with him. I can understand that.

'Women loved him and he couldn't help himself,' she says now. 'And I was never beautiful, but I always had a lot of spirit.'

It slightly breaks my heart to hear my nan say that now, although it is without an ounce of self-pity. I've seen pictures of her when she was young, and she was very cute, with blonde curls, green eyes and a fantastic figure, the tiniest waist I have ever seen. She has always had the naughtiest smile and minxy nature.

I think she is still incredibly beautiful now. Then again, maybe that's because we have a thousand in-jokes, she's looked after me all my life, prays for me every night, and seeing her laughing and enjoying herself – as we do constantly when we are together – is the loveliest sight I can think of. How can I not think that she, and all of these special women, are breathtakingly beautiful?

For their first date, Jack took Nan on a tour around the

sights of central London. He paid a cab to drive them around all afternoon. Nan presumed he was very rich; he was actually pretty much broke, but had happened to have a good win on the horses and thought he might as well use it to impress her.

This is a terrible gene that all of his descendants, me included, seem to have inherited. Even when I can't afford to switch on the heating and am secretly living off lentils, whenever I go out I find myself buying rounds for strangers, insisting on getting shots for everyone, taking unnecessary taxis and generally behaving like some sort of crazed oligarch. Everyone in my family does it and none of us can quite explain why. I have spent many mornings of my life fishing out receipts from the bottom of my handbag and wondering how I can have racked up a two hundred quid bar bill when I'm miles away from payday and I only meant to go out for a quiet Sunday lunch. I blame Jack.

Anyway, of course Nan became even less interested in her nursing course, as she soon began escaping back to London every chance she got so that she could hang out with Jack.

At almost exactly the same time as Nan met Jack, Rose went to a dance at Chiswick Town Hall, where she met a dashing former Air Force pilot called George. He was from East London and had flown Lancaster Bombers during the war.

Around the same time that Rose got engaged to George, Nan had to drop out of her nursing course at the age of nineteen, because she was pregnant.

Present Day

Of all the Indian dudes we meet on our travels, the one we become friendliest with is Ravi. He is one of the few guys we have encountered who is kind to us without being a total creep.

'Like Ravi Shankar, the famous sitar player!' I couldn't help exclaiming delightedly when he introduced himself, even though it occurred to me that loads of people must say this exact same thing to him when they meet him. Or at least, loads of annoying hippie white girls visiting Goa probably say this to him when they meet him.

Ravi works in one of our favourite shacks on the beach. It's the one we go to the most because they have sun loungers that you can hang out on all day, even if it's only in exchange for a couple of lime sodas. Getting Nan and Rose down to the beach is quite a performance, so once we're there, we don't want to move. At least not until snack time, which is by the hotel pool every afternoon at four o'clock. Every day there is a different ice cream flavour, and they alternate between bhajis and pakoras (both with a particularly good mint sauce). They are delicious and, most excitingly, free.

On the days we are hanging at the hotel, we stuff ourselves at breakfast then go straight through to the free four o'clock snacks. I invariably go up to the little beach bar and request four ice cream cornets while filling a huge plate with bhajis or pakoras.

'They're not all for me!' I add cheerfully, every single day, as if they even care.

But, before snack time, many hours are spent at the shack with the sun loungers, where Ravi always takes a lot of care in setting up our umbrellas for us and making sure we have a stack of towels.

Ravi and I get to chatting, particularly as I am often on the beach by myself while the others are deciding what to wear and Ann is reading her book by the pool. He tells me he is thirty-four and not married, which seems quite old to be a single guy hanging around here. All of his siblings are married, but he has resisted so far, apparently. His family are farmers in Shimla, which is up in the Himalayas and very cold in the winter. So, Ravi spends six months every winter working on the beach in Goa, and the other six months back home working on the family farm.

My nan and Rose went to school for a time in Shimla and are delighted to hear all about the place. Their school has a different name now, but the building is still intact. Nan's face lights up as Ravi describes what it looks like and they realize they are both definitely talking about the exact same place. He is delighted, like so many people are, by Nan's grasp of

Urdu and her knowledge of obscure Indian oddities that no westerner would usually know about. The two of them roar their heads off with laughter while discussing a childhood game called *goolie dunder*. Apparently it's like rounders. Ravi assures my nan that he is a champion at goolie dunder.

Ravi is a man with a slight air of mystery about him. He has a pleasantly battered boxer's face, with a flattened nose that has clearly been broken more than once. He has a large tattoo on one bicep and a gnarly-looking scar that twists all the way down the other arm. He likes terrible dance music. One day he disappears into town and comes back with a new spiky red-tinted hair do.

'I think he might be trying to impress you, Ells,' notes Ann.

Every day, he'll come and sit on the edge of my sun lounger and chat. His English isn't great, although he also speaks a smattering of Russian, which is rather impressive. It's always slightly awkward without Nan and her Urdu skills, so our conversation mostly consists of him asking if I'm OK and me saying yes, thank you, repeatedly. If anyone else comes over to talk to me, usually the water sports guys that I have also got friendly with, who always seem to want to take selfies with me, he hovers and looks menacing until they go away.

He's always inviting me to come to the beach party with him and I always say no. I never tell him how old I am and I guess he must be working on the common assumption that I am an extremely haggard teenager, because every time, I tell him 'my grandmother won't let me' and make a sad face for good measure. Family pressure seems to be something he understands, as he never hassles me about it. I have to admit, it's very relaxing having this as a ready-made instant excuse. Nice as Ravi is, I barely feel tempted. I'm too ensconced in my routine of bed before midnight and early morning yoga.

I never make it to any of the beach parties, although I can hear them sometimes from our balcony. I chat about them with a young hipster Russian couple on the beach one day – they have just arrived and want to know what people do for fun around here. When I mention the beach parties, they turn their noses up – it's all just drugs, they say. They've heard the beach parties are 'terrible'. Then again, they have come via Mumbai, which they keep telling me is 'a total shithole'. They have found Goa marginally preferable so far, but they're still not sold. They wish they hadn't come to India. Next year they think they'll go to Tulum instead. Of course.

Although I keep turning down his beach party invitations, Ravi is extremely kind to my nan and aunties, which makes me feel very fondly towards him. He cannot do enough for them, hugs them all every time he sees them (while nodding formally at me), and generally goes out of his way to be a good guy. Every day, he asks us if we're coming back for dinner (which we sometimes do), and if he doesn't see us for a few days because we're off travelling, he gets worried.

He doesn't have a car but he doesn't like us having to walk home along the beach, so he always gets his friend to give us a lift along the back road back to the hotel, or finds us a tuk-tuk. He helpfully suggests it might be more comfortable if he gave me a lift on the back of his moped, and we meet the others back at the hotel, rather than trying to fit four of us in a tiny tuk-tuk. Every time, my nan shakes her head firmly and insists I cram into the front with the driver.

'Oh, let her go with him, Dot!' Ann says. 'She's a big girl. You know her mother would be on the back of that moped like a shot – and so would you if you could!'

Ann and I both agree that while Ravi is not exactly attractive *per se*, there is something interesting about him.

As well as his kindness to old ladies, we are particularly taken with his affection for animals. The ubiquitous dogs that roam the beach are not bothersome and look fairly healthy, but they go largely ignored. Nan is not a fan of them and continually tells me off for getting too close. They can be a bit intimidating because they roam around in large packs and we can hear them howling at night, but they are always friendly. It's easy to forget they're there – there is always a dog lying under my sun lounger that I forget about and step on whenever I get up for a swim in the sea. They take it in good humour.

Ravi has adopted one of the stray beach puppies and dotes on her. He has bought a collar for her and christened her Lucy.

'She is my little darling,' he tells us.

This battered-looking, tattooed beach dude gets pretty sappy around Lucy the puppy. I don't blame him. She is very sweet. I spend hours playing with her and Nan tells me off for letting her lick my face.

On our last day, I go down to the beach by myself for a few hours, while the others are packing. It pretty much goes without saying by now that their packing would take about ten times as long as mine. I have shoved all of my belongings into a suitcase, and even with all the hippie tat I have been amassing by the day, there is still room to spare. I'm not sure what the others are doing that takes so long.

So I use the time to have a last swim in the sea, lying on my back with my eyes closed and the sun shining on my face. It's easy to float in the Arabian Sea and it's warm as bathwater. It seems impossible to imagine what late January at home is going to feel like in less than twenty-four hours. Ravi brings me a beer and asks where the others are.

'They'll be coming down for lunch in a little while,' I tell him. 'They're packing. We're leaving tonight.'

He makes a sad face. Then he tells me he has a break coming up, and maybe we could go for a walk down the beach together. It's my last day and Ravi is probably the closest thing I have to an actual friend in India.

'Sure, why not?'

Ravi grabs two beers from the bar and says something to his boss that I don't understand. He puts the beers in my bag and we walk down the beach. We walk silently for a little while, and I find I don't really know what to say to him now we're alone. Once we're quite a way down the beach, he starts to veer away from the shoreline, into some scrubby land behind the beach that has the odd shack and cow in it, but no people.

'Where are we going?' I ask.

'I show you a place to stay. If you come back next year. Without the family. I tell my boss I show you.'

He points to a wooden building in the distance.

'Is that where you live?'

'No, I live on the beach. Sometimes I go there to sleep. I show you. This way. Not far.'

I'm instantly cross with myself for agreeing to this walk in the first place. I don't want to wander into the wilderness with this man, or see some dodgy cheap accommodation where he will probably murder me. It's incredible how quickly I assume that a man's going to murder me.

'If I get murdered, please note it was probably Bad Boyfriend,' I've been saying to friends lately, only half joking.

It would be ironic if I came to the other side of the world to 'find myself' or whatever, and managed to get myself murdered by an entirely different man in the process.

'I'd rather not, actually,' I say out loud. 'I don't really need to see any accommodation. I'd like to stay on the beach. My family will be here soon.'

'OK. Up to you.'

He shrugs, perfectly good-naturedly, and I remember again how kind he has been to my family, and how sweet he is with Lucy. I feel a bit silly for assuming he was a murderer only seconds ago.

We sit down on the edge of the beach in silence. He opens two bottles of Kingfisher with his teeth and lights a filterless cigarette without offering me one. We drink our beers in more silence. I drink mine quickly as I find I'm a bit bored and want to go back as soon as I politely can.

I guess I thought we might become friends, but the atmosphere has turned awkward. Although our previous chats consisted of a lot of nodding and smiling, I felt like we got on quite well. As soon as we got out of sight of his workplace, he seems to have changed.

I try and fail to think of something innocuous to say, just to start any kind of conversation. So I smile and drink my beer.

I don't even know if I'm surprised or not when he suddenly lunges and kisses me. It's a fairly chaste closed-mouth kiss that tastes of particularly strong cigarettes and disappointment.

I'm a tiny bit cross with myself – what did I think was going to happen? Still, what a depressing way to have to think. I don't want to think this was inevitable. I don't want to have to assume that all men who are kind to old ladies and animals must have ulterior motives.

After approximately two seconds of modest, closed-mouth kissing, Ravi tries unceremoniously to jam his hand down the front of my dress and bikini top.

I am done with this experience. It makes me realize I'm kind of ready to go home.

'My grandmother will be wondering where I am,' I say primly, leaping up and walking back towards the bar.

'I know, I know . . . you're a good girl,' Ravi sighs.

He doesn't add 'but you can't blame a dude for trying'. He doesn't need to. I feel mildly fraudulent. He probably thinks I'm a virgin.

When we come back into plain sight, Nan, Rose and Ann

have arrived at the bar and are setting themselves up on sun loungers.

'There she is!' Nan calls out. 'Over here, Ells!'

'Where have you been?'

'Oh, nowhere.'

Only Ann smiles knowingly.

Present Day

Every day when we've been on the beach, Rose has been longingly eyeing up the parasailing going on down at the watersports shack. It's visible from all around – a bright striped parachute sailing through the sky, attached to a speedboat.

Rose has always loved anything to do with flying – it's no coincidence that she married a former RAF pilot. During her adventurous younger days, she used to hang out at the Bombay Flying Club. A boy who had a crush on her, trying to impress her, once took her up in a two-seater plane, flying out over the sea and doing a complete loop-the-loop. She adored it. She only found out later that he must have *really* been trying to impress her, as he didn't have a full pilot's licence and was not qualified to take her up alone. As with so many things, even at the age of eighty-eight, Rose still notes she did not tell her mother about this, or she'd have been in trouble.

She loves anything to do with speed and adventure; she has always zoomed around on her own steam, ever since learning to drive when she was in the WACI. She recently took her advanced driving test – she wanted to make sure she was still up to scratch as she drives her grandchildren to and from school each day – and passed with no faults.

Every day, we watch the colourful parachute billowing in the sky and Rose says how she wishes she could go up there. I'd be able to tell she was looking at the parachute even if I couldn't see it myself, just from the wistful expression in her eyes.

We do some research and – not altogether surprisingly – find that she isn't able to go parasailing. She's in pretty good nick, but her mobility isn't brilliant. More to the point, it's not covered on her insurance, which was difficult enough to get to start with.

She takes this on the chin but it's a disappointment. There are some significant downsides to getting older, obviously. It's rubbish being the person with the most knowledge and experience, and being told that you're not allowed to do things.

That's when Rose decides that I should do it instead. *Someone's* got to do it, she reasons. We're not going home missing out on this opportunity entirely.

'Up, up and away,' she whispers to me at fairly regular intervals throughout our holiday, just to remind me that this is definitely happening.

She instructs me to find out the price from the watersports boys on the beach, and then she slips me the money. We wait until the last day for me to do it, the others poised to watch me. Nan of course is mildly panicked by the situation and isn't convinced it's safe. Ann volunteers to film it on her iPad, while the others find a comfortable bench in full view of the beach.

I go down there first thing in the morning, preparing to get it done. The watersports guys tell me to come back in the afternoon, maybe about two o'clock. That's when the wind is best for parasailing.

I go away feeling a bit twitchy and anticlimactic. It's funny, I was never wild on the idea of parasailing before. Now I am anxious to do it. A bit nervous, even though none of the elements involved are things that I am nervous of.

On holidays when I was a teenager, it was always Stepdad and I who would do these sorts of activities together, while my mum and my sister watched from a safe distance. He and I would go jet skiing, water skiing, kayaking, whatever. With him I never once felt nervous about it. I always felt looked after.

I loved having our little gang of two. When time went on, we would go on family skiing holidays where my mum, sister and K would form 'the spa gang'. They would go and have massages and facials in the hotel spa, or spend the day hanging out and chatting in the steam room, while Stepdad and I went skiing, just me and him and a hipflask.

I can't dwell on this for too long, but maybe thinking of him doesn't make me as sad as it used to.

I go off and lie about on the beach for a while, then I go back to the watersports guys in the mid-afternoon. It's still too early, they tell me, the wind's not right. Come back maybe at four, five o'clock.

None of these smiley, chatty watersports guys seem to have any sense of urgency about this. They have been good-naturedly hassling me for days to go out on a boat with them or do some sort of sea-based activity. Now that I want to, they don't seem particularly fussed about whether I actually do or not. I have been out with boys like this.

By about half past four, conditions are apparently OK. The wind has whipped up and is blowing in the right direction. I duly go down onto the beach in my bikini and Ann accompanies me, ready to film the whole great adventure on her iPad. Nan and Rose are watching from a distance. I wave at Rose, wishing she were able to come up with me.

I feel strangely nervous as I am strapped into a life jacket, with loops that will attach to the parasail. Later my mum will watch the video on Ann's iPad with a raised eyebrow: 'is it really necessary for *five* of those boys to help you into that life jacket, Ells?' It's possibly excessive. They all seem to be hanging around, and I hope the spectacle of me trying to go parasailing isn't going to be too amusing. Then an English photographer from Bristol turns up and asks if he can take pictures. As always in India when there is anything going on, a small crowd begins to form, and random strangers take pictures of it all.

I then have to spend a lot of time standing around, while they test the parachute and wait for the speedboat to turn up. We can see it on the horizon; it's miles away and doesn't seem to be speeding particularly quickly in our direction. After a while, my nerves turn to boredom, and I'm not sure which is preferable.

Mostly I stand around feeling slightly self-conscious, wishing I had brought my sarong with me. Eventually – thankfully – we're ready and I am strapped in, attached to the parachute, which is attached to the boat. A man in a Bob Marley T-shirt, whose name I am not told, will be accompanying me up and steering. He's behind me, so I get the full panoramic view of the coast below.

And so we go up – up, up and away. There's only a second of frantic running along the beach, like something out of *The Flintstones*, before my feet leave the ground. We are up there surprisingly quickly and surprisingly high. At first, the wind is rushing in my ears and it feels like we're moving at the speed of light. Or at least the speed of, like, a fast car or a motorbike or something. I hold onto the ropes while the dude behind me has his bare feet wedged into the middle of my back. It's surprisingly reassuring.

Once we're up there, at full stretch with the parachute behind us, everything falls quiet. It's very, very still. I am never still. I am surprised at how peaceful it is. I am floating silently.

We can see for miles and the sun is just starting to set beyond us. I feel very, very high up. My friend behind me points out a shoal of black fish, hundreds of them in formation.

It feels like meditating. Or, rather, it feels like I wish meditating felt. I am very bad at meditating. My brain being this quiet is a rare occurrence. It feels like we're up there for hours, but it's only a few minutes.

I never want it to end. I marvel at how liberating it feels for everything to have fallen away. Money problems, boys, existential angst . . . how much does any of it really matter, anyway? I feel fully myself, up here. I feel, as they like to say, like *enough*.

And it's long enough, I realize. I can't stay up there forever; it has to end eventually. I will have to return to my real life. But it's OK. I've had some time and things have got better. I can take this feeling with me. I am ready.

While we are still all the way up there, above India, I do a little salute to Rose. A literal salute. She can't see me from all the way down there but I do it anyway.

Present Day

When we organized this trip, I anticipated it would be a great and interesting experience, but – to be perfectly honest – I expected to have had enough of being around family and to be ready to come home by the end of it. I am fairly used to living alone by now and my tolerance levels are not notably high. I'm quite set in my ways by this point.

However, now the end is upon us, I could honestly stay longer. I'm not sick of sharing a room with my nan; in fact, I'm genuinely going to miss it. Of course, I'm going to miss doing yoga every morning and having my breakfast made for me and generally living in this luxurious manner, but most of all I am going to miss hanging out with these incredible women every day. I am going to miss them terribly. Even as Nan and Rose inexplicably take around six hundred hours to pack their suitcases, long after Ann and I have finished doing ours and are hanging out on the balcony, drinking coffee and waiting for them – I will miss all of this.

Of course, on our last day in India, everything takes on a

predictable but special significance. Packing up our stuff feels a bit sad. We have got used to living in these rooms. We have got used to our routine. It's a really fucking nice routine.

At my last yoga class, I smugly note that I can pretty much pre-empt every move now and do the advanced version of everything. I am sure that when I go back to doing occasional yoga on the floor at home, along to a free YouTube video, I will hear a stern voice in my head commanding 'RELAX YOUR ENTIRE BODY, RELAX ENTIRELY'. I hope so anyway.

I consider trying to talk to the teacher at the end of the class, telling him it's my last day and thanking him for all these days of yoga classes while I've been here. However, he looks very preoccupied and I chicken out at the last minute. I hope maybe tomorrow he'll notice my absence, since I have been there at the front of his class every day for weeks now. Somehow, I have a feeling he won't. He must see an awful lot of people exactly like me passing through. I find this thought strangely comforting as I lollop back to the room in my old Prince T-shirt and grey gym shorts for the last time.

Of course, our final day requires the breakfast to end all breakfasts. Nan has been reminding everyone repeatedly that it's our last day, and we are given the absolute prime outdoor umbrella table. We sit there in the sunshine for hours, while I methodically stuff myself with my favourite breakfast dosa and sample pretty much everything else available from the breakfast buffet.

The Crow Man never looks at anyone nor acknowledges anyone's existence. We wave at him as we leave, even though we get no response. It seems fitting.

While the others continue their packing-up mission, I agree to meet them for lunch, then go off and do the rounds of my village friends to say goodbye before I leave. It's kind of a mixed bag, I've got to say. I don't kid myself that I'm anything special; again, they must see a lot of people like me come and go.

While Sonia says a tearful goodbye and brings her daughter out to bid me farewell too, Priya is furious that I am leaving without being talked into having my hands hennaed. I try to explain without offending her that it just won't look cool once I get home – despite my deep love of India, I really don't want to go back and become one of those terrible clichéd Brighton white people with braids in their hair and stupid tie-dyed trousers on in January. She still gives me the proper stink-eye when she realizes I'm actually leaving without being talked into it. She's done with me.

'I hope you will come back,' Sonia says, hugging me. 'You don't have a husband. Perhaps you will come back here for your honeymoon.'

'Perhaps,' I say hopefully.

'You have a boyfriend. He is a good man, yes?'

To be honest, I've lost track of who I've told what. In some situations here, when I've been put on the spot and felt vaguely uncomfortable about it, I've lied and said that I'm married, my husband is at home. Even in a vague lie like that, it feels odd even to say it. I wonder if I'll ever get to say 'my husband' for real. The word feels foreign in my mouth.

Some of the time I've hedged my bets and said I have a boyfriend back home. My thoughts flicker briefly to The Lecturer. He's the closest thing I have to a boyfriend; I'm in touch with him every day, after all. But I know I'm not really entitled to call him my boyfriend. I smile at Sonia and hope maybe she's right.

'I think you'll be back next year! For your honeymoon!'

This actually makes me feel oddly optimistic even though I'm certain she is incorrect.

I've got so used to being here, it seems unthinkable that I will soon be at home. I walk through the village a last time, hot sun on my back and my feet dusty as I walk down the dirt track, and home seems so far away I can barely remember it. The colours, the sounds and the smells here just seem so much more exciting. I can't believe that I'll be going back home, where there are no cows in the road and food doesn't have a hundred delicious spices in it, and everyone's clothes are not in bright colours and beautiful fabrics. The palette at home is just so much more muted. The light is not as bright. I try to breathe in every last bit of sunshine and spice and joy that I can, while I wave goodbye through the village.

Our flight is late in the evening, so we manage to squeeze in lunch, afternoon snack and dinner before we go. I want to get as much sunshine, sea swimming and Goan curry into my system as is physically possible before our departure.

Checkout from the hotel is technically at midday. Considering our quite high-maintenance requirements, we have requested a late checkout and the manager has said that she will try to organize a room for us somewhere in the hotel, so we can have a shower and a sit-down before we leave if we need to. She will let us know whether there is a room free as soon as she can, although she won't be able to confirm until the last minute. We say we'll come down to reception at the official checkout time.

Just before the allotted hour, there is a knock at the door. It is RJ, Nan's hotel boyfriend. He looks oddly shifty.

'I came to say you can stay in these rooms,' he says quickly. 'You don't need to move or check out. It would be too much inconvenient for you. I have brought you a new key card, as yours will have expired.'

'Thank you, RJ!' Nan says. 'You didn't need to come all the way over here to tell us. We were just about to come over to reception.'

'No, madam. Don't go to reception. I have arranged this privately so you will not have to pay a late checkout fee. Just don't tell the manager. I have enjoyed meeting you very much. I wanted to make sure you were looked after.'

I am not surprised at this reminder that my nan is, basically, magic. However, I do tell myself I should have realized sooner that RJ was genuinely her friend.

'Excuse me, miss,' he says to me after the others have hugged him goodbye at length. 'I would just like to say something to you. I would like to say I have so much respect for you. I have seen you while you have been staying here, and how much you love your grandmother and your aunts. A lot of people of our generation, they don't appreciate their older family members like they should do. I have the greatest respect for all of you. Your family relationship is really very beautiful.'

He shakes my hand and leaves before I can say anything in reply.

Good old RJ.

Present Day

We have our last dinner in the exact same spot that we had our first meal on our first day, in what has become our favourite of all the local beach shacks.

Once again, I have a 'Go-go Goa' cocktail in front of me. I've got used to the taste of fenny, the strong and distinctive local hooch, over the course of our trip. Ann has a 'Goan Sunset', her favourite of all the local fenny cocktails. Nan and Rose, of course, stick with their usual gin and tonics.

'Well, girls – we did it!' Ann says. 'I wasn't sure what to expect, but it's been fabulous. Thank you all for your company. Cheers!'

As it's our last day, we have a couple of rounds of cocktails before dinner. Then Ann and I split a large bottle of Kingfisher beer, which I will miss doing every day. I order a Goan prawn curry, which I have eaten for nearly every meal the entire time we've been here. It's served everywhere, and unlike the more exotic local dishes like xacuti and ambot tik, it's usually just listed as 'curry'. Ann has the same, and Nan has tandoori chicken because she has it every single day.

I can't remember what Rose ate for her last Indian supper, but it will have been something bizarre and spicy, as she is the most adventurous of us all. In India I have eaten street food and shark curry, but I have nothing on Rose. She will order stringy-looking mutton vindaloo and whatever the hottest thing on the menu is, just because. Rose has the most incredible appetite for spicy food. She orders dishes that waiters will always warn her are far too spicy for Western people and possibly even for most locals. Perhaps she would like to order something else.

'Make it as spicy as you like, darling,' she will say, in the manner of a drunk man in a curry house late at night.

So, of course they do, and Rose will calmly and happily eat it without so much as breaking a sweat. Every dish also must come with the Rose special on the side: a bowl of sliced raw onion.

As we eat our last Indian meal on the beach, our first day here feels like a lifetime ago. As well as being a lot browner now and wearing a ridiculous kaftan from a market stall, I feel different. I feel genuinely peaceful; I feel like I have really had a break. I'm also looking forward to getting back to work and seeing my friends – a sign that I must be doing at least some things right in my life.

When the time comes to leave, I'm glad for once that Nan and Rose can't walk quickly. We all savour that last slow walk back across the beach.

I actually find myself tearing up as the staff wave us off when we leave to get onto the bus to the airport. Miraculously, nobody is sick on the bus this time. Doing the same journey in reverse, everything is familiar now. It would be easy to forget how unfamiliar and exotic it looked when we arrived.

Like last time, we are driving in the dark, but I can pick out all the landmarks this time around, still illuminated by fairy lights. We go past the yoga shack, through town, past Café Ganesh, where whatever the time of night, the roads are busy with mopeds and cows. Rainbows of fairy lights flash past my eyes as we trundle down the uneven roads.

We don't really get to savour the final sights, as the driver of this bus back to the airport is certifiably terrible. A seriously bad driver, even for India. Many of the drivers we've had over the past weeks have been, but this is next level. We speed into oncoming traffic as we join the main road out to the motorway, ascending to top speed even as we bump over potholes and the inevitable debris in the road.

In fact, due to the driver's inexplicable hurry, we make it to the airport in record time. Our flight isn't until 2 a.m. and we have hours to kill. Despite this, everything gets so rushed that it becomes a total blur.

Even though I feel I've got somewhat used to being in India, being back at the airport is a culture shock. I thought it would be easier on the way back as I have grown more relaxed and accustomed to the general pace of life. No. Not at all. The airport is utter mayhem that I will never be accustomed to. My head spins the minute I set foot off the bus. In fact, I don't think my feet hit the ground.

Nan and Rose are immediately hustled into wheelchairs and two men push them towards the terminal as if they're racing, while another grabs all of our suitcases. Ann and I are sprinting to keep up. We follow them as they rush through the vast airport corridors, into mysterious service lifts and, for no good reason, straight to the front of the long immigration queues. At one point, the suitcase man goes off in a different direction and I follow him, losing the others and panicking.

After all that inexplicable hurrying, they despatch us in the departure lounge, right next to our gate. It is almost deserted and we have plenty of time to spare. Still, these random men – I have no idea whether they actually work at the airport or not – seem very pleased with themselves for getting us there so unnecessarily quickly. So much so, that apparently the money I pay each of them is not nearly enough. Nan thinks it's more than fair and instructs me to ignore them. I don't have any rupees left, so I give them the English money I have in my purse as well. They tell me this is a bit of an inconvenience, but it will do.

It's only when I get home and do a little bit of research that I find out the unofficial porter culture in India is a tricky issue. Did these men actually work for the airport? No, not really. They were obviously pushy and maybe even a little bit threatening, but with a lot of suitcases, they were also undeniably helpful.

I know there are lots of people who are against encouraging 'coolies' (which is considered to be a derogatory term), and there are lots of reasons not to indulge in the heavy tipping that I have felt necessary. There are many conflicting arguments on the subject. Not to mention that sometimes the ambush of 'help' can feel intimidating. However, I would admittedly have been a little bit lost without it.

So, now we have time on our hands in an airport where there is really not very much to do. I have a look in the duty-free shops but, having grown accustomed to beach life, am shocked by how commercial and overpriced everything seems to be. Oh God, I really am going to go home as one of those people with stupid trousers and braided hair. I am my own worst nightmare. My friend David used to go out with this annoying girl who claimed to have lived in a cave for a year, and she once spent an evening showing me her photographs of the time she 'went travelling' in India. Her photographs all showed her wearing a sari and hugging people who looked as though they didn't want to be hugged. Oh God, that's going to be me.

Just for something to do, I pick up a box of ladoos to take back for my office. They are not particularly delicious sugary Indian sweets, but it's the thought that counts. When I get to the till, the lady informs me they are the equivalent of about fifteen quid. I put them back.

With time to kill, I do laps of the large departure lounge, marching in circles.

'You always have surplus energy, don't you?' Rose notes, as I walk past and wave to her for around the tenth time.

Nan spends the time making friends with the bathroom attendant, a thin wan-looking woman whose job is to hand out paper towels. They talk for so long and so deeply in

Urdu, we practically have to drag Nan away when our flight is called.

When we eventually board the plane, the flight home is far more subdued than the outward journey was, as return journeys tend to be. Ann drinks red wine and watches *Rebel Without a Cause* while the rest of us sleep on and off. Nan doesn't even wake me up or interrupt my films once. We fall asleep arm in arm, and I feel very grateful to be there with her.

As always, I'm in awe. If I'm tired out and over-emotional, I can only imagine how she must be feeling.

When we wake up, it's at a cold and rainy Gatwick Airport, early on a very grey morning at the end of January. It doesn't seem right somehow. The adventure is over.

It feels surreal when we say goodbye in the exact place we convened weeks ago, at the rainy taxi stand. I wave the others off and make my way to get the train home. I miss them already.

October 1951

When Nan found herself unexpectedly pregnant at the age of nineteen, Dolly and Chum immediately said to her 'it's all right, just come home'. Grateful and relieved, she did exactly that.

She and Jack had a quick wedding and he moved into the family home, too. Everyone seemed to live in that house at some time, whether because they had been dumped, got pregnant, or were saving up for a place of their own.

When Nan's best friend Penny also found herself unexpectedly pregnant a couple of years later – and she found out her boyfriend was actually married and had no intention of leaving his wife, and her parents weren't nearly so understanding about her situation as Nan's were – Penny moved in as well.

Nan said she had so little idea of pregnancy and childbirth, she burst into tears when her waters broke and her mum had to explain to her what was happening. Still, she was delighted to give birth to a baby boy.

Ann and Sam, Nan's two youngest siblings, were still only little – so everyone pitched in and helped look after each other's babies. It sounds like my idea of heaven – I'd love to have a baby and move back in with my mum, quite frankly. Grey Gardens, here we come. Dolly and Chum loved having a house full of people, and they would all have curry together round the kitchen table on Sundays, with the kids sitting on boxes and the bin when there weren't enough chairs to go round.

Nan and Jack were very happy together for a time, and had a second baby four years later, my mum. However, he couldn't deal with family life and my nan was left to bring up the children by herself.

She still mostly remembers his handsome face and his kind, easy-going nature, rather than how difficult this must have been. He and my nan stayed on good terms – even slightly romantic ones, although they no longer lived together – until he dropped dead when he was only in his forties.

It must have been incredibly hard to be a single mum in the early Sixties, but Nan was never bitter.

'Bringing up my children was an utter joy. I wouldn't change a thing. I'm grateful for my husband, because my children took after him and they are wonderful.'

She used to dread having to go to things like school parents' evenings, as it was so unusual for a woman to be alone at that time. She now says she wishes she had gone out and met someone else while she was still young, but it never occurred to her at the time – she was exhausted. She was asked out a few times, but she never said yes.

She never did go back and finish her nurse training, although she says if she had really loved it, she would have found a way to do it. Not working for a living was never an option, though – so after she had the baby, she went to a job interview at Ealing Town Hall, having applied for a job as an audiometrician, giving hearing tests to schoolchildren.

Her pal Susie got the audiometrician job, but Nan impressed the doctor who interviewed her with her brightness and was asked if she would like a job as a community health administrator. It was a job where she thrived; she spent all of her life working in public health and social services, and she loved it.

My nan always stayed around West London. She and her children eventually moved out of the family home and into a rented flat in Ealing. Nan was eventually able to buy the flat herself, as well as her house in Spain. When she retired, she moved to a bigger house and to be nearer to my mum, a bit further west outside of the city.

Rose and George moved out to the countryside, where she got a job as a school secretary and became an excellent golfer. Rose was fourteen years into her marriage before she unexpectedly got pregnant. She and George stayed together until he died a few years ago, and she now lives in a big house in Dorset with her son and his family, where they all have a great time.

Ann, both much younger and 'the bright one', was the great hope of the family. She was terrified of telling her parents when she accidentally got pregnant at the age of twenty-one. The first person she told was my nan, who had been through the exact same thing.

Ann still managed to train as a teacher while she had a baby, had one more, and then had a fabulous life living all over the world. She and her husband made a very glamorous couple. She looked after him when he became ill and died much younger than he should have. She now has a flat in West London, near where they all grew up, and a house in Cyprus. Both of her children live in Australia and she spends a lot of time out there. She spends all of her time being fabulous.

None of their lives turned out the way they thought they would. All of them are happy. All of them consider themselves lucky. Not least because we all have each other and we all get on so well. It's quite an achievement, really.

'Just look at where we started and where we ended up,' Nan says now. 'I'm so very proud of all of us.'

It's easy to look at older people, especially when they have children and grandchildren, and to assume that their lives were always smooth and predictable. This is almost never true. Everyone has had hard times; everyone has had their heart broken. Nobody gets everything they ever wanted. If we're lucky, life is long enough that it all works out in the end, somehow.

I try to bear this in mind when things don't go my way, or it feels like a run of bad luck might be endless. For better or worse, things can change in a minute. Who knows where we'll all end up? They certainly had no idea at times. So . . . might as well try to ride it all out and stay staunch.

Present Day

I come back from India, not into normal everyday life, but into something straight out of *I Capture the Castle*.

Months earlier, before the India trip had been booked, my girlfriends and I had decided that we needed something to look forward to in January. We booked a long weekend in a Landmark Trust house: Wilmington Priory, overlooking the Long Man and less than an hour's drive outside Brighton.

When Nan booked the India trip, I realized that the two almost coincided. Fortunately for me, I was still able to do both, but I ended up with approximately two hours at home between getting in from Gatwick and my friend Emma coming to pick me up to go into the countryside.

The booking confirmation for Wilmington Priory warned us that there was no central heating and the parking space was a walk away from the house. This was for hardy travellers only. And so, I dropped my suitcase off at home, put on two jumpers and my wellies, and shoved some thick socks and extra layers into my rucksack.

'You are the dictionary definition of the word "trooper",' Em said, as she picked me up and saw my jetlagged face.

I hadn't realized I looked quite that bad, but I guess I have missed a night's sleep and was, to put it kindly, somewhat disorientated. Despite my suntan, when I am very tired, my face goes pale and puddingy. We all have our tells.

We pick up Natalie, and we meet Saoirse on the way, at Waitrose in Lewes, where we stock up for the weekend. I reflect that our grocery shopping choices reflect the in-between space we currently occupy in life. I mean, when I was younger we didn't used to shop in Waitrose when we stocked up on the way to Glastonbury – I guess we are coming up in the world. We still buy far too much booze – more wine, gin and beer than four people should be able to drink over the course of a long weekend (and still Saoirse and I will have to do an emergency extra booze run to downtown Seaford by the second night, because we got over-excited and drank it all too quickly). But, on the other grown-up hand, Natalie has made a list and we buy all the ingredients to make lovely family meals together: cooked breakfasts, a Saturday night chilli, Sunday roast lunch. We are growing up. Sort of.

It's the cosiest weekend imaginable. At times, I am so jetlagged and shell-shocked, I can barely string a sentence together. Fortunately, I am with such good friends that nobody minds. They have a million questions about my trip but I haven't processed it yet. All I seem to be able to say is that it was 'incredible'.

I get to have the bedroom that I wanted the most – luckily for me, everybody else thought it was too chilly and far away from the main house. Half of the priory is in ruins, and the rest is sprawling and ancient. There is still a secret passage (sadly, long disused) into the local church. We discover a secret cellar that is full of scary caverns and possibly bats.

My room is tucked away beyond the huge unheated hall that is now used as a ping-pong room. It has a little writing desk with a view of the Long Man of Wilmington, lying there in the rolling green hills.

It's all enough to short-circuit my brain. This time yesterday I was still among the smells and sounds and colours of India. The palette here is entirely different. I miss the reds and the spices and the chaos. It is so boring that there are no cows wandering around the roads, that people don't chat to you – or even look at, or acknowledge, you – as you walk down the street. Everything here seems so organized and prescriptive and bland by comparison. The vibe here is just not mystical at all. That's something I'm going to have to preserve myself.

I'm so glad I have come home to this, though. While in some ways the timing is ridiculous, in fact it could not have been better. I am so grateful to have this stopgap, to put off doing the washing and being in my damp house by myself. Here the atmosphere is green and lush and the countryside quintessentially English. I have come back to the best of it.

Also, I think it would have been lonely to have gone straight home alone after these weeks of camaraderie and excitement. I'm grateful for the company.

Mostly, I am grateful to continue to be around great women. I am with such good friends, they don't mind when

I shuffle about the house in my flannel nightshirt (it was a present from my aunt in Austria and it's the warmest thing I own), knitted American Apparel knee socks and a blanket at all times.

Still, I feel faintly guilty that for once I am not the life and soul of the party. I have a lovely time, but I feel quiet, slightly withdrawn. It's not my usual role; ordinarily, I would make sure everyone is having a good time all of the time.

Natalie does pretty much all of the cooking and I worry slightly I'm not pulling my weight, but I have to admit it's lovely to be looked after a bit. She has the most energy of anyone I know. We both wake up early every morning and have a couple of hours, just the two of us, drinking tea and reading our books on separate sofas in front of the fire in the grand Georgian sitting room. I love our time together: Natalie perpetually brims over with positivity and I love just being around her.

I am so grateful for these women. For Emma, who is the most solid and principled person I know. For Saoirse, who is endlessly empathetic.

We go for long walks, build fires, drink lots of wine, play board games and talk about anything and everything. It strikes me that we're not so different from my nan and her sisters, not really. I just like being around great women and hearing their stories.

For some reason that weekend – with a glass of wine, in front of the fire – I tell my friends a bit more about what happened between me and the Bad Boyfriend. It's the first time I've said any of it out loud, except to my therapist.

Over the previous months, my therapist has gently questioned me on my reluctance to talk about this; she worries that I don't have the support I need and that I'm keeping it quiet because I am somehow ashamed of myself over the whole situation.

'Why should you be the one to carry this?' she asked me. 'Are you the one who has done anything wrong? Did you spit in *his* face and call him a whore for no reason?'

I have to admit that, no, I did not.

When I tell my friends about what happened, I am taken aback by how shocked and upset they are by it. It reminds me that however much I make jokes and try not to think about the whole thing too deeply, it was actually pretty bad.

'I'm so sorry that happened to you,' Natalie said.

'I can't believe it,' Saoirse said.

'I want to fucking kill him,' Emma said.

For the first time, I don't try to play it down or make it into a funny story. I'm glad I have told them. These women are on my team and I don't always have to play a role or make everything fit my fuck it's cool, everything's great narrative.

It is not embarrassing to be struggling sometimes. It's OK to admit it – which, up until now, is not something I have been doing.

I've made some questionable decisions along the way, but it's not all my fault. For me, it's just been circumstantial, a pile-up of stuff and a run of bad luck. It's nothing to be ashamed of. I decide not to be, any more.

Present Day

Then, the following weekend, The Lecturer comes to stay.

I am so excited to be seeing him again. While I've been away, we've been texting every day, a constant conversation that I always look forward to continuing. Every time I saw anything interesting in India, or some tiny funny thing happened, I couldn't wait to tell The Lecturer. Basically, I live to amuse him. He's so world-weary and sardonic, making him laugh feels like winning the lottery. I fear I've become a bit addicted to it.

It's been a long road for me and The Lecturer. It's been on and off, full of grey areas and misunderstandings, and things left unspoken. For a long time, he was such an enigma to me. However, while I've been away these past few weeks, I have become convinced that this is going to be the turning point. All obstacles have receded; we are both single. We have been growing closer and talking to each other about *everything*. Also, I have come back from India really feeling myself, what with the suntan and the daily yoga routine. How can he resist, right?

Preparing for a visit from The Lecturer is a military operation that requires careful planning. He is highly fastidious, a fussy eater, with unusually keen observational skills and an unabashedly critical eye. He doesn't miss a trick. It makes me very self-conscious around him. As such, my house and I are both required to be in immaculate order before he arrives.

Although he claims to have no friends and no social life, it's always hard to pin him down to a date and he has actually only ever come to stay at my house once before. I have never been allowed to set foot in the flat where he lives. He always makes the same joke whenever I ask him about it: his landlady has two rules, no prostitutes and no kebabs (so I'm barred on both counts, ha ha). Obviously on hearing this I always laugh and pretend I don't care about the fact that I am not really a proper part of his life.

He claims that I am his favourite person to spend time with, yet he never comes over. Last time, I tried to impress him in the morning by making him a bacon sandwich while wearing only Agent Provocateur lingerie. Surely every man's dream, right? He barely gave me a second glance and then told me off because I used the same chopping board for the bacon and the bread. The Lecturer is something of a germophobe and finds my lack of rigorous kitchen hygiene very painful. He likes to joke about how this is his abiding memory of that entire experience, and that he still has nightmares about it. I have to admit, it's pretty funny the way he tells it, but it's not brilliant for the old self-esteem.

So, this time I want things to be perfect. Then he can get on with realizing he's madly in love with me and can't live without me, obviously.

The Lecturer drives down to Brighton in his rickety old car, which I adore. It's somehow always covered in mud and looks more suited to a grizzled old farmer than a long-haired academic who lives in London. Then again, The Lecturer is always surprising me. It's one of the intriguing things about him. Just when I think I know everything about him, he'll casually throw into conversation that time he lived in the rural Australian outback, or made a living playing in a swing band, or was a teenage athletics champion.

In retrospect, I suppose these should all have been red flags, warning me against this unknowable man. But for over two years (on and off), the drip feed of these random facts just seemed fascinating.

'You look like you're planning a kidnapping,' I say as I run outside and he gets out of the car.

Characteristically, there is a length of rope, a box of ammunition (not *quite* as sinister as it sounds, he's into clay pigeon shooting) and a bottle of champagne visible within the utter tip that is the boot of his car.

'Shut up,' he says in his brusque Yorkshire accent. 'And come here.'

You have to admit, he has his moments, this one. This is what has made me persevere with him for so long.

He walks towards me with his arms outstretched and his eyes unusually soft.

'I haven't seen you in so long,' he says.

He has a pleasingly snuggly jumper on and he seems unusually glad to see me. Despite this, I don't kiss him even though I would really like to. I'm never sure if he wants me to. He does not kiss me and the moment passes.

Ostensibly, we have a lovely evening. We drink wine and we order dirty takeaway burgers. And we smoke cigarettes and we sing along to music and we sort-of talk about things. Except we don't really.

For months now, I've been saying all this indecision is not his fault. He's been having a hard time. He's had a strange and unsettled year. He went through a big break-up. He has left his job without another one to go to, and now he isn't sure what to do next.

He talks in vague terms about moving to the countryside and writing a book. He has offers for other high-powered academic jobs that he might or might not accept. He is considering chucking it all in and, at the age of almost forty, 'going travelling'. We both agree that is an objectionable term, and instead start referring to it as 'going for a wander'.

We are always manufacturing intimacy in this way; we have so many obscure words and phrases and nicknames for each other, it's practically a secret language. It is very seductive. Although he is an awkward academic who we agree is more than likely somewhere 'on the spectrum', as they say, he doesn't half know how to pull out all the classic fuckboy tricks that a million Instagram memes are built on.

It's all in-jokes and pet names, and he's always going on about how nobody understands him like I do. He says he finds it difficult to talk to people, so he doesn't understand why it's so easy for him to talk to me. This has allegedly never happened to him before. He tells me I know more about him than anybody else on the face of this planet. In short, he makes me feel special. It's only as time has passed and I realize I've constantly been fed this convenient and neatly constructed little narrative of Poor Awkward Socially Inept Lecturer and Special Magical Me that I start to wonder whether I have in fact been played by a major player.

He talks about his crippling awkwardness, his chronic indecision and his low self-esteem. Yet somehow he has managed to get a PhD and a series of high-flying jobs and sustain other relationships, just not with me. Sometimes I think he is clinically depressed. Sometimes I think he is just being stubborn. It doesn't really matter which. He certainly does not seem to want to be happy. I could make him so happy. I am convinced of it. Why doesn't he want me to?

For nearly two years I have been waiting. For his life to settle down, for things to get better. Mostly for him to realize he is madly in love with me. I don't understand why he says he's so unhappy and yet refuses to choose happiness. He claims that he thinks I'm wonderful and beautiful and brilliant, yet he knows he could be with me and he just . . . isn't.

So, we listen to Bob Dylan and eat burgers and drink more wine (and whisky, and absinthe). He has brought with him the small collection of vintage guitars he owns, the purpose being that over the course of the evening, I will help him narrow down which ones he should keep and which ones he should sell, as most of his belongings will be going into storage when he decides whether he is moving house or 'going for a wander'.

I tell him about India and about Wilmington Priory, although he already knows most of it because I have been texting him constantly and sending him pictures of all of it.

'That sounds magical,' he says. 'Your life is magical. I wish I had friends and fun and a lovely time like you do.'

You could, I think. I am literally offering you that. I don't know how many more times I can tell him this.

I tell him that my friends and I are planning to go back to Wilmington again in the summer, as we think it would be extra wonderful when it's warm enough to have cocktails and dinner outside in the ruins. There was even a grand outdoor dining table especially for that purpose.

'You should come with us!' I exclaim, undeterred as always. 'We were thinking of July, so obviously you'll be back from your wander by then. And we decided we'd let boys come next time.'

I'll wear a diaphanous 1930s dress. He will impress my friends with his intellect and his haughty cheekbones. We'll drink French 75s and sneak down to the bottom of the garden, where he will kiss me up against a tree and tell me how much he loves me and how lucky he is. It will be perfect. Obviously.

'Maybe. Who knows? I'm just going to go wandering until I get bored. I might be gone for a year, or maybe more.'

In all the time we've been talking about his 'going for a wander', we've never talked about timescales. It's never occurred to me that it might be for longer than a month or two at most. I feel so stupid, I don't even question the fact he might be going away for a year. I don't say anything and just pretend I knew this all along. Being the cool girl and constantly hiding your feelings is so exhausting sometimes.

Then comes the real kick in the teeth.

'I expect you'll have found yourself a real boy by the time I get back and I'll just be left feeling sad and regretful.'

He sighs extravagantly and his pretty brown eyes beg me to please feel sorry for him. Like he's Pinocchio or some shit, and he really doesn't get a say. He just can't help it; it's not his fault.

I suddenly – belatedly – realize that, even though he texts me every day, I am not part of his decision-making process at all. I am irrelevant. Finally realizing this for sure feels strangely good. It feels liberating. Sort of. Even if I do really, really want to cry.

I don't, obviously. I just make yet another shit joke at my own expense and ask him if he wants another drink.

This is a man who is going through life alone, I realize. He never sits next to me when he can sit on the other side of the room. We stayed the night together in a fancy hotel once. In the morning, he got out of the luxurious hotel bed where there was an adoring and reasonably attractive girl next to him, and positioned himself awkwardly on the window sill, saying he needed air. Even looking at him right now, idly playing a guitar along with the record we are listening to, it is evident he is using it as a barrier between him and me. I am sitting cross-legged on the sofa; he is hunched uncomfortably on the wooden floor and keeps batting away my offers of a seat next to me.

I hear Ann's voice in my head: 'Don't put your eggs in that basket, Ells. You're an attractive woman. You're still young. It simply shouldn't be this hard.'

The Lecturer and I go to bed anyway. Because . . . of course we do. I may be having revelations and epiphanies all over the place, but I'm still me.

I take off my clothes, down to the fancy underwear I have put on especially, and get into bed. He gets in next to me and I kiss him, knowing even as I do so that I should have made him sleep in the spare room. But I kiss him, knowing this is going to be the last time.

'If I'd known this was available on the menu, I should have done it sooner,' he says. 'I thought you were trying to have boundaries, or whatever it is you're always talking about . . . Are you sure you want to do this? Because I'm going away and I can't . . . I don't want to lose you as a friend.'

'Lecturer, we were never really friends,' I say.

From my end, at least, it's true.

I cry when he leaves in the morning because I don't think I will ever see him again. Then I go about getting over it, for real. I am done.

A couple of weeks later, I surprise myself by bursting into instant, physically painful tears on seeing a text from him that says, 'And now I'm in Vietnam'. That's it now, I realize. He is far away from me.

I cry as if my heart is broken, but it is not. Not really. I know what a really broken heart feels like, and this is not that.

But the thing is, I'll miss him. For over two years we spoke nearly every day. We sneaked off for lunches together that consisted of a bottle of wine and a bowl of chips between us. I wrote him notes and bought him little presents, and he never did the same for me, but doing it still brought me joy. I loved trying to cheer him up. We never did most of the things we planned to do (go to an auction, go on a road trip, go on a boat trip, go to Paris); admittedly they were all pretty much my idea, but I'm reasonably certain we both enjoyed talking about them. He made me laugh and he totally got my sense of humour in a way that very few people do. He gave me advice on my work and it was good, valuable advice. He took me clay pigeon shooting and, because it was with him, I actually unexpectedly had fun. We would have remote film dates, where we'd both press play on a crap horror film at the same time and text each other our critiques throughout.

He made me feel like I was in a cool little gang of two. Drinking pink cocktails and smoking sneaky cigarettes and telling secret stories on a balcony overlooking a pretty corner of London on summer evenings, while we laughed at each other's jokes and bitched about everyone else – it wasn't real intimacy, or a real relationship, but it felt great.

It may have been misplaced, but I loved him. I'm not sure he really knew, even though I was always telling him. However, if there is one thing I have learned recently, it's that I can't keep flogging a dead horse like this. It's no way to spend a life, at any age.

I can hear Nan's voice in my head, obviously. I have

always been both utterly baffled and totally admiring of my nan's ability to compartmentalize. I have always thought perhaps it's a generational thing; Rose has it as well. People of that age have seen so much shit, I think they've had to develop it as a survival tactic. Otherwise they would all have gone around dying of heartbreak all the time. However, those two definitely take it to extreme levels. I will never forget my complete shock as they told me, totally stony-faced both of them, about how they feel nothing for their father. He hadn't been at all interested in them, and had chosen not to be involved when they were growing up, why would they waste a moment's thought on him? They had their mum and the most wonderful stepfather, not to mention each other.

Rose walked past him in the street once. When she was an adult, years after she'd last seen him. She was working in the City and he walked past her when she was out on her lunch break. She told me they made eye contact, recognized one another, then both carried on walking.

'And how did you *feel*?' I cried dramatically. I was clutching my heart, my voice ringing with emotion. Admittedly I'd had more than one glass of wine, but even if I hadn't . . . Well, this little story makes me feel *a lot* of feelings.

I have no idea how I would feel now if I walked past Stepdad in the street. I do know, however, that the answer would not be 'nothing'. I feel physically panicked at the thought.

'I felt nothing,' Rose said, as if she were surprised by the question. 'Nothing. Why should I?'

Nan nodded in agreement. Both staunch and unwavering. They went on to change the subject to *Poldark* or something, while I remained open-mouthed in amazement and still experiencing a lot of feelings at this revelation.

Nan has often tried to coach me, in recent years, to channel some of this spirit. In the most part, I'm afraid I have failed miserably. I am incapable of switching off my emotions, of compartmentalizing even the tiniest thing. I'm sort of proud of it – in fact, sometimes Nan's calm logic and 'forget about it' attitude frustrate me terribly.

I am the opposite, and I kind of like being neurotic and emotional. I have sleepless nights over missed opportunities and minor arguments I didn't win. The marvellous French expression *l'esprit d'escalier* (the wit of the staircase – or thinking up the perfect response long *after* a conversation) could have been invented for me. I'm constantly reliving situations and thinking about what I could have done differently. How I could have been better.

'What you have to do,' Nan instructs me in her calm voice, as if she's stating an obvious fact rather than the impossible, 'is think *can I change this by worrying about it*? If the answer is yes, then great. If the answer is no, then do not waste your time.'

I am in knots. I am worrying about everything. This is fucking ridiculous.

'How?' I ask her. 'How the hell do I do that?'

'You just get on with it,' she says. 'You do other things. It's hard sometimes. But you do it.'

Usually at this point, I would lose patience and start raising my voice, talking to her like I'm still a stroppy teenager, saying it's all very well for her, but *I* can't do that. I'm an emotional person. I'm a fucking writer, for goodness' sake. If I can't feel all my feelings long past the point when it's healthy or useful, then who even am I?

Instead I decide to listen and do my best to take her advice. If she can do it, why can't I? She's been through a lot fucking worse than this. Ironically, it occurs to me that The Lecturer would surely approve of her logic, but obviously I don't ask him at this point. You can't really ask for someone's advice on how to go about getting over them, much as I would actually like to.

That ship, I decide to decide, has sailed.

So, I cry for half an hour on my sofa, and then I delete The Lecturer's text and go about trying to 'do other things'. It's hard. But it sort of works. Not totally, because that's not possible. But mostly. And that's not too bad.

Present Day

My nan and I are agreed on one thing: that we both disagree with this modern obsession with 'getting over it'. Getting over it is *not* the same as getting on with it. It's a phrase that is used so often, and that I hate. Why should 'getting over it' always be the aim? Why is *not* being 'over it' something to fear at all costs?

I have been through some things in my life I will never get over. At the very least, I will be different because of them. But it's more than that. There are some things I will always be sad about. And that's OK.

My nan is in her late eighties and she has a brilliant life and she, for the most part, regrets nothing, but there are some things she has carried through her life that she will always be sad about. That's OK. She has lived life bravely and fully. That's the price you pay.

Yeah, you can get on with it. Nobody's saying you can't. In fact, you *should* get on with it as best as you can. You can be fucking staunch about it, but some things will still always be there, underneath. Always.

That's all right.

I'm quite happy where I am (full disclosure: I'm drinking a glass of wine and listening to Elliott Smith at my kitchen table as I type). I'm OK. I'm at peace, but I'm not *over it* and I never want to be.

Unfortunately, I am also of the opinion that you can't be friends with exes. Not really. In an ideal world I would like to be, and I think all of mine are extraordinary humans (we're excluding Bad Boyfriend from this particular generalisation), but I'm not sure I can consider any of them real friends.

K and I tried, heroically. We have been through so much together. God, we grew up together, really. We both want the best for each other; we wish each other well.

Sadly, it turned out we cannot be friends. We tried going out for drinks, then when that didn't go well we tried going out for coffee. That also didn't go well. We are incapable of seeing each other's faces and not crying. Last time we met up, we ran into a girl we know, who sweetly and obliviously came rushing up to our table to say hi. Her friendly expression turned to horror when she slowly realized that we were both weeping hysterically. We couldn't stop, even while we tried awkwardly to explain ourselves. If we're not both crying, then we argue over whose fault it was and how fucking futile the whole situation became. It's just not healthy.

So, at least we both know ourselves by this point, even though it's a shame. Every year, when it's his birthday, I feel a bit sad. We spent so many of them together. By this point, I actually don't try to fight myself on this. If for one day of the year in particular I allow myself to feel sad about the demise of an often-beautiful relationship that lasted well over a decade, then so be it.

Sadly, no matter how much we went through together, I can't say I count him among my friends at this point.

Maybe I'm just not that evolved, but mostly I think it's because I can't stand the sadness that such stepping down inevitably means. I look at the beautiful faces of these incredible men and it blows my mind that we could once have been everything to each other and now we're just . . . not. They knew me so well. They have seen sides of me that nobody else will. What does that even mean now? Where did all go? Does it still exist, somewhere? My poor brain simply cannot take it.

I'm OK with remembering the good bits, but I just can't be confronted with the evidence that life has moved on. The smallest details slay me, anew, every time. I only have to see K wearing a coat I don't recognize and it makes me want to kill myself. He once didn't own a single piece of clothing that I wasn't intimately acquainted with. Now we have nothing.

I don't know if it makes me an idiot, but I feel the same about my stepdad. He's not my father. We are not blood relatives. If he is not married to my mum then what are we to each other?

He will always be the man who brought me up, who taught me to drive, who helped me with my maths homework. Nothing will change the fact that he was the first person ever to play me a Prince song, and it changed my life. He went to great trouble to get hold of *Rumble Fish* on VHS so that we could watch it together and it blew my fucking pre-teen mind. I miss getting his advice on things as an adult. I miss him taking the piss out of me and I can hear his chuckle now as I think of it. I miss him.

But the thing is, I know there is no possible alternative.

If we did have a relationship, what could that even look like? What would we do? Go to the pub together for a couple of hours before he has to go home to his house I have never been to, where he lives with his girlfriend I never want to meet? Am I supposed to betray my mum and break her heart in exchange for, what, lunch a couple of times a year and a birthday card if I'm lucky?

Fuck that. Maybe it's my problem – wanting nothing if I can't have everything. But for me, personally, there is no alternative.

There are things I will forever be sad about. There are songs I love that I will never be able to listen to again because I can't bear the memories.

So, yeah – apparently there are some things I will never *get over* and I am totally at peace with that.

August 2017

My brief relationship with Bad Boyfriend left me with a lot of things, none of them good. Mistrust of other humans. Self-esteem in the bin. Endless self-recrimination. Total lack of faith in my own judgement. However, shortly after that, I finally picked up the phone and rang a therapist who had been recommended to me by a trusted friend. I was trying so hard not to cry, I could barely speak. I knew I should have done this much sooner, but it was my experiences with Bad Boyfriend that finally convinced me to do it.

My therapist's name is Kathleen. I made an appointment to meet her at her office, and I have sat in that room for an hour a week ever since.

I've had therapy a few times before in my life. I've never stuck with it for very long. A few times, I've been in crisis and seen my GP, but by the time I've made it to the top of the waiting list for a proper psychiatric assessment, the moment has passed and I don't want to waste anyone's time. It's the accepted belief in my family that I probably have something 'wrong' with me, but I have never been formally diagnosed.

The thing is, it takes very little to make me suicidal, but then it takes very little to make things seem bearable again. It's such a rapid cycle I can barely keep up, but it means it's easy(ish) to keep going and just get on with it when the perfect storm has passed.

Also, I've never found a therapist I've really, properly clicked with before. I've been to see a few that are so wishy-washy I find it difficult to respect a word they say, and I want to roll my eyes aggressively every time they utter 'and how does that make you *feel*?'.

The last one I saw was a strict, austere middle-aged woman with a pleasingly unplaceable European accent, like some sort of generic Bond villain. She was fond of a smart jacket and silk scarf combination, even though her practice room was in her grand seafront apartment and we had to walk through her kitchen to get to it.

She was of the opinion that psychotherapy was supposed to be hard, and she would bark at me for an hour every week and then give me homework. It was only when I realized I was dreading our appointments all week and usually cried during the walk there that I decided not to go and see her any more. She was quite cross with me when I told her.

The minute I walked into Kathleen's office, I knew she was my kind of person. I know you shouldn't judge on first impressions, but I liked everything about her: her face, her voice, her outfit. She looked kind. She wasn't much older than me, but she sounded like a woman who knew her shit. I trusted her straight away.

She calls me up on my tendency to turn everything into a funny story, but we still have a laugh. By this point, I don't even feel too awkward crying in front of her. And please do bear in mind, I am a *very* ugly crier. Seriously, it's gross. One of my great delights is when I make Kathleen swear, which happens from time to time ('I'm sorry to say it, but it sounds like he's being a fucking twat', for instance. Hi, The Lecturer).

I have told her things that I have never said out loud to a human being before, and I have never regretted it once. When I first went to see her, I was at a low ebb. However, I wasn't in crisis. I hadn't been for a while. It was just that things weren't really getting better – there's a difference.

For the first time, I was serious about breaking some patterns and genuinely changing my behaviour. I didn't want to keep going on like this. It was the most committed I had been to my mental health, the first time the idea of 'self-care' had ever gone beyond the occasional urgent need to save my own life.

Fortunately, it just so happened that I had come to the right person. Every week I look forward to my hour on a Wednesday afternoon in Kathleen's office. She doesn't take notes, or make me take my shoes off and lie on a couch. She doesn't try to talk to me about 'mindfulness techniques', and I love her for it. Thankfully she never gives me homework that consists of listing 'fifty things I like about myself' or similar. She just lets me talk, and sometimes she chips in and says things I hadn't thought of, which usually make perfect sense.

She makes me look at things differently and I try my hardest to bring this attitude out of her office and into my real life. I have become more tuned in to how I feel around other people, and as a result I try to be around people who make me feel good. I think about how I communicate with others and the effect I am having on the world around me. In tiny baby steps that may not even be visible to the naked eye, I am getting better at speaking my mind and standing up for myself.

If you asked anyone who knew me a bit, they would say that I was outspoken and fearless. I fart in public and make dick jokes and speak my mind at all times. Except, the people who really know me would add that I use this as a smoke-screen to hide the fact that I'm actually terrified of people's opinions of me. I pretend I don't care because I care too much. I do it with work, I do it with boys I like. I'm embarrassingly frightened of people not liking me. I am embarrassingly frightened of failing. I'm even more frightened of the slightest conflict.

I talk to Kathleen about this, a lot. We unpick a lot of things and I say things I don't expect to say. I've been feeling things I never even noticed before.

A few months in, I started to worry that I was just talking a big game – as I always do – but not actually making a change. I was recognising the things that were not OK, but still chasing after indifferent boys, still saying yes to things I didn't want to. Just like how I like to shout loudly and publicly about feminism and fuck the patriarchy, but then I shocked myself by being unable to speak up when Bad

Boyfriend liked to choke me and threatened to 'beat the shit' out of me.

Deeds not words, was what I kept telling myself. But it was hard. Kathleen kept reassuring me that it takes some time and effort to break lifelong patterns, and that I was doing pretty well in taking the first steps. I was trying. But it never felt like enough.

Then, something shifted. Kathleen said my intuition about people actually seemed to be pretty good, but I didn't always like to acknowledge my own gut feelings. I would notice the red flags but ignore them, as if pretending they weren't there would make them go away. I would make excuses for people and impose my own fictional narrative that would make it all OK.

With her help, I'm starting to see things more clearly. The passive aggression of The Lecturer seems so obvious now, I can't stop noticing it. For a while, he would still send me the odd plaintive text message from amid his 'wanderings'.

'I miss our pointless idle chats,' he says. I am furious. He can't even say he misses me without belittling our entire relationship. To me, it was never pointless. For a while, it was everything.

'I don't understand what you get out of this relationship,' Kathleen said to me once. 'Do you think you can try to explain?'

I couldn't.

But slowly, I feel like my decision-making is getting better. I think about things before I automatically say yes – some of the time, at least – which is a huge breakthrough for me.

I am still working towards being one of those self-possessed people who is able to say 'no' really firmly yet gracefully – like my nan, Rose and Ann, basically. I might never quite achieve that, but at least I am trying. I truly believe I am becoming more staunch, and will continue to do so. Staunch wasn't built in a day but I'm getting there.

I don't fall to pieces when The Lecturer and I are finally over. I don't spontaneously fuck someone else unsuitable in some sort of obscure 'revenge' that he will never even know about. This might not sound like a huge triumph, but it actually is.

I only got together with Bad Boyfriend in the first place because I'd been unceremoniously rejected by The Lecturer the first time. Then after Bad Boyfriend, I had this sudden feeling that I didn't want him to be the last person I had slept with – so I went out and slept with a grubby sort-of ex at the soonest possible opportunity, his one major selling point being that at least I knew he wasn't actively scary.

I don't suppose that means I can blame The Lecturer for what transpired between me and Bad Boyfriend, but he certainly didn't help. In fact, when we started seeing each other again, I told The Lecturer eventually (a bit of) what had happened in the interim. At first, he made all the right noises and I was touched.

'I had no idea. I . . . I can't believe it. I always assumed you could look after yourself, you seem so strong. I would never have guessed I could feel so . . . protective towards you. *I want to kill him.*'

He hugged me and I leant against his chest feeling mildly

guilty and unfeminist for rather enjoying this uncharacteristic little outpouring.

Then, later in the evening, after a few cocktails: 'But you have to admit, you are pretty damaged. I guess I'm not totally surprised. Oh, don't look at me like that – we're both fucking damaged. It's why we get on.'

I think I was supposed to find this funny.

Anyway, I don't do anything terribly self-destructive in the wake of The Lecturer. I miss him horribly. It leaves a hole in my life, of text messages and company and attention and in-jokes, if not the proper relationship I thought it was, and I don't rush to fill it with the first thing that comes along, just for the sake of it, which is a first.

I hang out with my brilliant girlfriends as much as possible. I work hard. I throw myself into writing. It feels good.

'You get a therapeutic gold star,' Kathleen tells me.

I try just to stick with it – hold steady, stay staunch – and for the first time I succeed. I have lived alone for over two years now. At first I hated being single and now I like it. I can live with myself quite happily, for the first time ever. I have been stable for a while now.

I guess at some point I might not need her any more, but I'm not sure. I'm not thinking that far ahead, yet.

Present Day

Of all the incredible women I am blessed with in my life, of which I am lucky enough to have many, my stepmother Fiona is up there as one of the best.

When I come back from my trip, she calls me with an idea. She and my dad (well, it was all her idea; with the best will in the world, and my dad is wonderful, these sorts of things are rarely Dad's ideas) would like to put some money into helping me fix my crumbling house. I could cry with relief, and I do.

Dad and Fiona offer to come and stay while the work is done, and we can do some of the other jobs I've been putting off while we're at it. It is like a huge boulder has been lifted from my mind. I know how lucky I am, and having a parent who can offer to do this for you at the age of thirty-six is a ridiculous spoiled privilege, but this is the kindest and most helpful thing anybody could possibly have done for my mental health.

I've been losing a lot of sleep over the past few years over the damp problem in my kitchen. I think water is coming in from outside, but I can't figure out how or from where. A couple of years ago, a guy came and looked at it and charged me a few hundred quid to be rude to me and staple a bit of something over the outside wall. Unsurprisingly, it seems to have made no difference. I have been at a total loss as to what else I can do about it, so have just been feeling quietly overwhelmed ever since.

One of the kitchen walls is slowly crumbling before my eyes. It's started to turn black with mould, which is more than a little worrying. I've covered up the worst of it with a poster of Mexrrissey (Mexico's premium Morrissey tribute band), which I nicked off a wall on a night out. But the wall is so damp it can't even hold the weight of this cheap bit of A2 paper. It's forever falling down in the night, waking me up and giving me a fright with its weird swishy noise, and every time bringing another clump of plaster with it.

I haven't been sleeping well at night since the Bad Boyfriend, anyway. After he disappeared, I started noticing things that were missing from my house, or had been moved into strange places. It's all unsettling enough that I haven't been feeling safe in my own home, yet have also felt paralysed about what I can do to fix it.

The kitchen floor is the main problem. It is covered with nasty grey Seventies lino, which was there when I moved in and I have never taken it up for fear of what is underneath. The floor feels very uneven underfoot, and there is a whole section by the back door where it feels as though there is nothing underneath the lino. I tried taking that corner up once, just to have a peek, but it was rotten and smelled like death so I just pretended it had never happened and vowed not to think about it again (good Nan skills, there). When I have parties I have to ask people not to stand by the door. I'm convinced that either I or someone else is going to fall through the floor and break an ankle, although that is a small fear compared to the one about how my house is probably falling down on its foundations with every passing minute.

My friend Jem lives two doors down from me and had a similar problem. When they looked under her floor, there turned out to be a rancid black lagoon and some deadly fungus under there. They had to take up the entire floor and rebuild the joists. She and her husband had to move out for two weeks while they got industrial dryers down there.

I ought to get mine looked at, she said. I can't afford that kind of shit, so I just continued to catastrophize and would wake up in the night, dreaming the house was falling down around me.

My dad and Fiona drive down from North Wales on a Sunday afternoon. They bring their own bedding, a lot of gardening tools and cleaning products, a couple of bottles of wine and a cheese board. Fiona has also brought some of her old Seventies records that she thought I might like.

We have booked in a nice man called Martin, a damp specialist who sorted out my friend Ari's flat when actual rainwater started running down her sitting room wall. Indoors. Compared to that, he says, this will be a piece of cake. He tells me not to look so worried, this house has been standing for well over a hundred years and it's not about to fall down now.

I start to feel better immediately.

Over the next two weeks, Martin and various members of his family – a couple of sons, a stepson, and most delightfully, his brother who is a dead ringer for Ronnie Wood – take up residence in my kitchen. They pull up the floorboards and do all sorts of other things. In the evenings, Dad and Fiona and I sit in the middle of the building site, drinking red wine and trying to come up with the ultimate Rock 'n' Roll supergroup (cue much discussion of Keith Moon versus John Bonham as drummer – I favour the former, although I do acknowledge the 'style over substance' argument here). I have to do the washing up in the bath. I'm so happy.

During the day, we take loads of old crap to the tip. We do three runs to the tip. I love the tip. We paint all of the outside walls and window frames. We plant spring flowers in pots. We hang up pictures that I've been meaning to hang up for months. I get paint on my jeans and haul bags of compost around and feel like a real person.

'I've had an idea,' Fiona says one evening, as we drink red wine and move onto bass players (Kim Deal or Kim Gordon, surely – all bass players should be called Kim).

Fiona's ideas are the best ideas. She recalls that, for as long as I've lived in the house, I've said I don't particularly like the front door. It's clunky and painted a kind of dull burgundy colour. While the builders are here, she reckons it wouldn't cost too much more to get them to stick in a new front door.

So after they've replaced twelve floorboards, installed new gutters and rebuilt the walls, Martin and his mates put in a new front door. It's the perfect symbolic gesture. This is my house now. A new threshold.

'You're a lucky girl,' Martin says, on his last day. 'You've got a really lovely dad and stepmum.'

I get quite emotional when he leaves. I'm not sure whether he realizes what a huge thing he's done for me. I've grown very fond of Martin and his family and I'll miss having them around. I've spoken on the phone to his wife Wendy so often, she's bought a copy of my most recent YA novel and gives me updates on her progress.

After my dad and Fiona and the builders have gone, I get to do the fun stuff that's left. I paint the kitchen pink and put up new fairy lights. My mum says she'll chip in as an early birthday present and springs for some handmade Mexican tiles with stars on them. I put a brightly coloured Moroccan rug down over the new wooden floor.

'This is the happiest kitchen I've ever seen,' Alice says when I have friends round to christen it.

Best of all, I paint the new front door a bright turquoise that makes me feel jolly every time I come home. I get to use the Greek door-knocker I bought in Hydra all those years ago, which has been languishing in a drawer ever since – the same door-knocker Leonard Cohen had on his Greek house. Well, pretty much.

Fiona buys me a new keyring with an 'E' on it to mark

this auspicious new beginning. I now have a kitchen that none of my previous boyfriends would recognize. I have a floor that Bad Boyfriend has never, ever walked on.

I burn some sage for good measure and close the new door on the world. I decide that I'm not going to let anyone in for a while.

Present Day

You will remember that when I was thirty, I decided I wanted to have a baby – exactly like every basic bitch in town does when she turns thirty. Now I'm nearly thirty-seven and I still do not have a baby.

When I told my friend Ari that K and I had essentially broken up because I suddenly wanted to have a baby, she said: 'If I were you, I might have had some sort of fertility test first. It would be ironic – after all this – if it turned out you were barren.' I burst out laughing and didn't stop for about ten minutes.

Although I now believe that things between me and K worked out the way they were always supposed to – we just weren't as happy or as well suited as I had once thought – I couldn't help but admit that she made a very good point.

The funny thing is, that crazed impulse to have a baby as soon as possible has gone away. I still think it would be nice, if it happened one day, but that horrible feeling of abject panic, of time slipping through my fingers, has receded. In some ways, I feel younger now than I did then – I don't feel frightened that my life is over any more.

If I really wanted to have a baby by any means possible, I could have done it by now. It's not that hard. I probably could have got accidentally-on-purpose knocked up by Ravi on the beach if I were really that desperate for a baby.

Back when K and I were in the midst of the painful, drawn-out process of deciding whether we should stay together or not, I decided that I never wanted to make any decisions based on fear. I can't think of anything more depressing. Surely nothing good can come of it. If I am to be remembered for one thing in this life, I want it to be for living bravely. I want to be brave, always. It's hard sometimes, but it is the most important thing to me.

I still feel that way, fortunately. It's something for me to hold onto, these days. Because the older I get, the more tempting it would be to make decisions driven by fear. The older I get, quite frankly, the scarier life is, in many ways.

The great hope I've got from hanging out with the older generation is that maybe the fear won't last. Hopefully it will come full circle. We can afford to be fearless in our youth, then obstacles come up and doubts set in – and then hopefully we get more staunch and overcome them.

It would be so easy to panic at this point. To think I had to find the first willing dude, get myself knocked up, stat. In short, to settle for less. But I'm not ready to do that and I never will be. I am incapable of settling. Sometimes that's far from being an admirable quality, but in this case I think it serves me well. However it works out, I am OK with it.

I have been madly in love in my life, and I have been loved. I have always had an army of family and friends around me. I am passionate about my work. I am excited about life.

Looking at the women around me, of every age, nobody's life has turned out exactly the way they expected it to, one way or the other. But it's always ended up being OK, somehow. You adjust. You get on with it. You get bloody staunch.

When you're going through a hard time, being told to keep things in perspective is not helpful. It's just really, really annoying. It's like someone in the street telling you to smile, or saying 'cheer up' as if that has ever actually made anyone cheer up.

But perspective was exactly what I needed and it was what hanging out with older women taught me. We all know it's too easy to look at everybody else and think they have their shit together and we don't; that rule applies even more when we compare ourselves to older women – especially if they have children and grandchildren, we assume their lives have always taken the conventional path, that their lives were so different from ours.

And in some ways, they were. Their lives were so different from mine that I can scarcely believe we have all existed within the same lifetime. But we are all the same. We have all had our hearts broken. We have all swallowed disappointments, big and small. And we have all experienced deep joy for no good reason and laughed in the face of it all.

Yes, our lives are all so different. Yes, sometimes I look at myself in the mirror and remember I'm in my late thirties and I look like a mum, yet somehow I am not one. That's a lot of good motherhood going to waste right there, I think.

I spend a lot of time these days reading articles about women who have 'failed' at many desperate years of IVF and who have now made their peace with being child-free. I like to listen to stories of fabulous older women saying they had a brief period of baby madness in their thirties, but it faded into a distant memory along with their hormones, and now they never give their life decisions a second's regret.

Maybe I will have a baby one day. I might have a life with a wonderful husband and happy children, and the noisy messy home I used to dream of, where I am a fun, sexy mum and we run around on the beach together and take it in turns to pick a record to listen to with dinner and go around the table telling each other one thing we learned that day.

Or maybe I will have a life of passionate love and exciting travel and loads of sex in European hotel rooms. It might be art and writing and cocktails and fascinating women. Maybe I'll live with my mum in her old age and we will get a lot of cats, which actually sounds very appealing.

It is all brilliant. None of it is perfect.

I mean, I love Sylvia Plath as much as the next over-privileged, mentally unstable white girl – but what I refuse to do is live my life according to that stupid, overused *Bell Jar* quote. The one where she pictures herself at the foot of the beautiful fig tree, paralysed by indecision and unable to choose just one fig, so she has to sit there and watch them all drop and go rotten at her feet. I'm sorry, Sylvia – but fuck that!

I'm becoming staunch. I'm getting stronger all the time. I hope soon I will catch up to my mum in the staunch stakes. One day I might even grow up to be as hard as nails as Ann, Rose and Nan. As wise, optimistic, fun, enthusiastic and bloody hilarious as those brilliant women I have had the privilege of spending time with. If I grow older with a fraction of their grace, humour and positivity, I will be very lucky.

So, in the meantime, whatever happens, I refuse to panic. I refuse to hurry. I refuse to be scared. What I needed to do was stop worrying and beating myself up over everything that had ever happened, and instead accept and fall in love with my destiny. I have come back from my trip to India with a bit of perspective on it all, and so that is exactly what I do. Whatever happens next, I am OK with it. Whatever it is, whatever it turns out to be, I choose to be madly in love with it.

Acknowledgements

Thank you as ever to the very staunch Caroline Hardman and all at Hardman & Swainson. Thank you to Rachel Kenny, Kate Fox and all the team at HQ.

As well as my travelling companions, thank you to my family and friends who feature in various guises in this book, especially my parents and my sister. Thank you also to those whose steady kindness and support did not make it into the drama of these pages, but helped me throughout.

Steve, I'm very glad I took one afternoon off when I was writing this book. To behold, look at all those chickens.

ONE PLACE. MANY STORIES

Bold, innovative and
empowering publishing.

FOLLOW US ON:

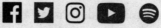

@HQStories